THE
CHRISTIAN-MARXIST
DIALOGUE

**Beginnings, Present Status,
and Beyond**

by
Peter Hebblethwaite

DARTON, LONGMAN & TODD

First published in Great Britain in 1977 by
Darton, Longman & Todd Ltd,
89 Lillie Road, London SW6 1UD

ISBN 0 232 51390 2

Printed in Great Britain by litho at The Anchor Press Ltd
and bound by Wm Brendon & Son Ltd, both of Tiptree, Essex

Contents

Preface

An author can sometimes have the gratifying and disturbing experience of finding that life catches up with him as he writes. Since I started this book, there have been a number of events that make the questions it deals with more pressing and urgent than ever.

First the 'Final Document' of the Helsinki Conference in July 1975 held out the hope that the relations between the two halves of Europe and the super-states of America and Russia would enter into a new period of fruitful interchange; but no sooner was the ink dry than there were complaints that the Conference had failed to make any practical difference in the East either to the free flow of information or to human rights. President Ford abandoned the term '*détente*' without shedding a tear. The Christian-Marxist dialogue described here was one expression of the high hopes of *détente* in its early phase. It made a not negligible contribution to an on-going story.

Secondly, the European Communist Parties have made considerable progress towards respectability if not credibility in the last two years. The Italian CP sees power almost within its grasp, and has strenuously worked towards the 'historic compromise' or possible alliance with the Christian Democrats. The French CP has gradually gained at the polls in coalition with the Socialists of François Mitterand. And both parties have risked the displeasure of Moscow by proclaiming their faith in democracy and pluralism. In both countries Christians have had to come to terms with this new language and decide whether to regard it as a true change of heart or a mere tactical switch.

A third fact of great importance is the way the balance of the Church's life has shifted to the 'third world'. Even if one does not embrace uncritically the thesis of Fr. Walbert Bühlmann, O.F.M., in *The Coming of the Third Church* (St Paul

1

Publications, England, 1976), his statistics make a significant point. Whereas in 1960 the Catholics of Europe and North America made up 51% of the total number, the projection for the year 2000 is that they will be reduced to only 30% while the remaining 70% will be from the third world. It does not take much imagination to grasp that where questions of hunger, poverty and social justice begin to dominate men's minds, the encounter with Marxists, also active in the same field, will be inescapable. The example of Latin America already proves this.

Christian-Marxist relations, then, are an important theme: they are also dangerously emotive. Already some violent pamphlets have been published which have generated more heat than light. One may mention for example Marcel Clément's *Christ and Revolution* (Arlington House Publishers, 1974) which sets out to prove the total incompatibility of Christianity with any form of 'Leftism', to demonstrate that 'socialism with a human face' is impossible, and that 'the Catholics who flirt with socialism are co-operating in man's loss of everything, spiritual and temporal'. His conclusions may be right, but they require a starting-point other than the assumption that 'Christian Marxists' are merely cretins or villains. Iris Murdoch once said that she was an ex-Marxist and an ex-Christian, and left her hearers to work out where exactly the stress should fall. In order to reassure readers who might be worried, I should like to say less ambiguously that I am a Christian who has never been a Marxist, and who does not expect or aspire to being a Marxist. My position is summed up in the words of Emmanuel Mounier, when he founded the review *Esprit*: 'We have agreed to state ever move clearly our intellectual differences with the Communists the more we draw closer to them in other respects'.

One practical note. Throughout this book I have taken the liberty of amending the translations from other languages where this seemed helpful. Opacity and jargon seem inseparable from the discussion of Christian-Marxist relations, but that is no excuse for unnecessary obscurity.

Wadham College, Oxford
1 September 1976

1
The Long Road to Dialogue

In the spring of 1967 I took part in a dialogue with a Communist, Dr. Arnold Kettle. The venue was a Friends' Meeting House, and the Quakers were visibly shocked by the Marxist notion that 'hatred' could be a force for good. But Kettle repeated that one had to *hate* the oppressors, and dismissed as so much well-meaning moonshine the idea that one could hate oppression while loving those who were inflicting it. The distinction seemed to him absurd—worse, idealistic. On the train back to London we had the real dialogue which had somewhat eluded us in the Friends' House. Kettle confessed that if he were to become a Christian, admittedly an unlikely event, he would become a Roman Catholic. He meant it kindly. I asked why. He said: 'Because you people have such a sense of organization'. I suggested that we had started to think of the Church not as an organization but as a communion, but as is the way of such discussions, he insisted that he knew better.

The idea that the Catholic Church and Communism are psychologically close to each other has been a cliché of the twentieth century. It is more usually a matter of blame rather than praise. Here, it is said, are two highly centralized and autocratic systems which cherish discipline in their members. Both have sacred books, infallible guides for the interpretation of new situations, and venerable relics. Both claim to cover the whole field of human experience: neither leaves anything out of its total synthesis. Despite their obvious competitiveness and hostility to each other, they are said to resemble each other like quarrelsome brothers.

This comparison makes the Christian feel deeply uncom-

3

fortable, but the sense of discomfort may be an indication of how near the truth it is. Only what hits the mark can really hurt. Thus in the summer of 1968 there were those who compared the encyclical letter, *Humanae Vitae*, about contraception and birth control, with the Russian invasion of Czechoslovakia. Of course, put simply like that, the comparison was absurd. No martyr burned himself outside St Patrick's Cathedral, New York to protest the encyclical. No tanks rolled into Nottingham to crush dissident priests. No bishops were sent to purge their guilt in distant forests. The Church may exercise authority, but it remains a voluntary society. The parallel with Communism as lived in Eastern Europe or China simply does not hold, and too many real distinctions have to be blurred for it to be even remotely plausible. The incompatibility between the Catholic Church and Marxism is more striking than any parallels that might be drawn. In the love-hate relationship, it is not love which has predominated.

A new fact has complicated the relationship still further. In a relatively short span of time some Christians have moved from a root and branch condemnation of Communism to an acceptance of it as the key to the understanding of history. In 1937 Pope Pius XI declared: 'Communism is intrinsically evil, and there can be no collaboration with it in any field on the part of those who want to save Christian civilization' (*Divini Redemptoris*). To qualify Communism as 'intrinsically evil' did not suggest that it could have any redeeming features. Yet by the mid-1970s many Latin American theologians were urging the formation of a 'strategic alliance' with Communism as the only hope for their exploited sub-continent. The purpose of this book is to explain, as far as possible, this surprising and for many disturbing development.

If the embracing of Marxism were accompanied by the abandonment of Christian faith, there would be no problem and nothing to explain: it would simply be another instance of 'secularization', this time in the socio-political field. But the fact is that in 1976 there are groups of Christians, small in numbers but not negligible, who are Marxists not in spite of their Christianity but *because of* it. They may, of course, be dismissed out of hand as thoroughly mistaken: either they have got their Christianity wrong, or they have got their Marxism wrong, or they have got both wrong. I do not take this *simpliste* view. The existence of such groups means that the theoretical question— Can a Christian be a Marxist?—has been answered positively: there exist people who are both sincere Christians and sincere Marxists. This does not prove that their synthesis is a valid one, any more than the fact that Christians have been racialists or women-haters proves that Christianity is compatible with racialism or misogyny. But is points to the existence of a problem which needs urgent examination. It has political, philosophical and theological consequences. Are the Christians Marxists heralds of the future or well-meaning but fundamentally misguided bearers of confusion? Are they prophets or dupes of propaganda?

From the outset a preliminary question has to be faced: which Marxism is in view, and how is it linked with Communism? Terry Eagleton, a British Catholic Marxist, has reminded us that 'in a world of Cuba, North Vietnam and East Germany, it would be self-evidently foolish to ascribe to Marxism a single, simple meaning' (*The Body as Language*, Sheed and Ward, London, p. 76). While self-evident foolishness must be avoided, the proliferation of Marxisms raises many difficulties. It is easy to find oneself talking at cross-purposes with a particular 'Marxist' simply because his vision of Marxism excludes more familiar forms. Few of the Christian Marxists have a good word to say for Soviet Russia or Eastern Europe: and that rules out one major field in which a more amicable Christian-Marxist relationship could reasonably be expected to improve the lot of the sixty million Roman Catholics who happen to live in Eastern Europe and have no option other than daily co-existence. Castro's Cuba has been more benevolently regarded and is held to have made an original contribution, but it hardly constitutes a distinct model, being heavily dependent on Russian influence. Occasionally eyes are lifted in fervent hope towards the China of Mao; but, as we shall see, few of those who speak so enthusiastically of 'the China experience' have any first-hand knowledge of that immense country. The Chile of Allende seemed a more promising candidate for the supreme accolade, but it was beset with difficulties from the start and subjected to severe political, economic and ideological pressures from the outside. By becoming the victim of 'Fascist oppression', it acquired the status of a splendid and tragic might-have-been. But Marxist Christians are not usually very worried by the absence of successful models of realized Marxism. They look to the future, and assure us that it will be very different 'next time'—more democratic and fraternal. They discourage crystal-gazing. Their model is deliberately 'Utopian'.

A further complication is that the precise heritage of Marx is a matter of considerable dispute among Marxists themselves. Should one oppose the humanistic 'young' Marx of the *Economic and Philosophical Manuscripts* written in Paris by 1844 and unpublished until 1932 to the 'classical Marxism' of the mature Marx which was institutionalized in the Soviet Union and which stressed the rigidly deterministic nature of his theories on society and human development? The 'young' Marx certainly displayed a more humanistic vision which is lost sight of in *Das Kapital,* but does that justify playing off the one against the other? This dispute over the inheritance of Marx was not merely an academic exercise, since, as David McLellan put it, 'for non-Stalinist socialists, the early writings of the young Marx could serve as weapons against the growing authoritarianism and bureaucracy of official communism' (*Marx Before Marxism,* Macmillan, London, 1970, p. 210). As the legitimating founding father, Marx has been put to many uses.

Nor did Marxism come to an end with the death of Marx. There is a 'development of doctrine' in Marxism. But that raises still further questions: there can be no doubt that Engels' version of Marxism was the crucial link in the chain that leads to Lenin, Stalin and Mao. But it was Engels who in works like *Dialectics of Nature* introduced the concept of 'dialectical materialism' into Marxism. Thus for some writers Engels became the villain of the piece. It was his fascination with the natural sciences that led Marxism to develop in the false direction of mechanical causality, and Marxism has found it difficult to recover from this lapse (Adrian Cunningham, *Adam,* Sheed and

Ward, London, p. 147). In the *German Ideology* Marx himself
had deplored all attempts at system-building and scorned all
merely speculative constructions. 'Marxism' thus turns out to be
an extremely slippery concept which eludes grasp and definition,
and there is some truth in Marx's only recorded joke: 'I am not
a Marxist'.

For all these reasons, the Christian response to Marxism
was not and could not be a simple matter. There is in Marx and
Marxism something for everyone. He can be benignly seen as
the first to draw attention to the terrible human toll taken by
the industrial revolution. 'The history of industry', he wrote,
'has not so far been conceived in relation to human nature, but
only from a superficial utilitarian point of view' (*Early Writings*,
Ed Bottomore, p. 162). Marx already had this 'humanistic'
approach at a time when Christians were hardly aware that a
problem existed, and some, indeed, were apologists for the factory system. Dr. Andrew Ure wrote in his *Philosophy of Manu-
facture*: 'There is in fact no case to which the Gospel truth
"Godliness is great gain" is more applicable than to the administration of an extensive factory' (quoted in MacIntyre,
Secularisation and Moral Change, p. 19). Marx was more per-
ceptive than most Christians in seeing that work had become
dehumanizing and alienating. This makes it easier to place
Marx in the long line of Jewish prophets who fearlessly denounce injustice and exploitation. However, this attractive interpretation ignores, or, more eirenically, 'puts into brackets' the
atheism of Marx. This remains a stumbling block for most
Christians.

For Marx was not only an atheist, he was the most radical
and thorough-going of atheists. He does not seem to have
known religious scruples or the twinge of *Angst*. Many nineteenth century atheists seemed obsessed by what they rejected:
the God they had discarded hung like an albatross around their
necks. Marx was not among them. 'To be preoccupied with
religion', he says curtly, 'is to fall into the error of the religious'
(Fourth Thesis on Feuerbach). It was an error he took pains to
avoid. At least where atheism is concerned, there can be no
question of contrasting the 'young Marx' with the 'mature

Marx'. In the 1844 manuscripts he developed the view to which he held firmly for the rest of his life—except that he gave it less and less attention. He envisaged a transformation of society in which man's needs would be so richly and fully satisfied that the very idea of a transcendent God would lose all meaning. And so too would atheism. Atheism, he says, is simply a mediating term which asserts the reality of man by the denial of God. He goes on: 'now Socialism has no need of such mediation . . . it is the positive self-consciousness of man, no longer mediated by the suppression of religion, just as real life is the positive reality of man, no longer mediated by the suppression of private property which is Communism' (1844 Mss). The atheism of Marx is thus complete, untroubled, serene, and *necessary*. It is not a *private* option but a social necessity. Marx had no use for the idea of the secular or lay state in which religion would be a legitimate private indulgence. 'The chief originality of Marx', writes Charles Wackenheim, 'lies in his denial of the specificity of religion. The questions raised by believers are not "real" questions: they are the translation of an unhappy, diseased consciousness' (*La Faillite de la Religion d'après Karl Marx*, P.U.F., 1963, p. 313). In suppressing the tensions which gave rise to such illusions, Communism would put an end to religion.

However, this does not entirely dispose of the questions of atheism, since 'Marxism' is not necessarily saddled with all of Marx's personal opinions. The historical question which then has to be faced was formulated by Professor Owen Chadwick: 'Was Marxism anti-religious because Marx and Engels were anti-religious? Or was their anti-religion an expression of an anti-religion which in no way depended upon their private views, but was (in some way still mysterious) necessary to the social aspirations of the working class?' (*The Secularization of the European Mind in the Nineteenth Century*, Cambridge, England, 1975, p. 74). Chadwick is much too canny an author to answer this question unambiguously, but he gathers a certain amount of evidence to show that some of the early communists had a Christian inspiration. The word itself is derived from a Christian memory, no matter how much it was 'deconsecrated' by Marx and Engels. The Magdeburg tailor, Wilhelm Weitling, was regarded by Engels as the founder of German Communism, and he was the author of *The Gospel of the Poor Sinner* (published in 1845). This Anabaptist firmly believed that *Christianity was Communism*, and composed poems for children in which he expressed his touching faith. One of them reads:

> I am a Communist child.
> Strong in my faith so mild,
> Because my God I know,
> To the Workers' League I go (*ibid.*, p. 77).

Weitling also presented Jesus as 'the First Communist'. In this tradition, the Churches were not blamed for following Jesus, but blamed for not following him sufficiently and faithfully. But this stream went largely underground until it re-emerged, here and there, in the 1960s. Marx himself had never for a moment entertained it.

Yet Marx's hostility to religion and inability to understand it did not prevent him from suffusing his work, for all its technicality, with a religious or even a magical glow. 'It (Communism) is the solution to the riddle of history', he confidently writes, 'and knows itself to be this solution' (*Early Writings*, 1963, p. 155). He calls for a commitment which begins to resemble faith and hope in the certitude it implies. He sees man as 'fallen', i.e., alienated, private property as the source of all subsequent evils, and the working-class as the bearer of redemption because it is the most evident victim of enslavement. 'Revolution' becomes the eschatological upheaval that will transform society utterly and lead to the paradisiac inauguration of the classless society. Marxism is a 'secularizing' force in that it has a this-worldly explanation for all phenomena: but it cannot entirely rid itself of ideas and a language that have their roots in religious experience.

This helps to explain why Marxism has exerted such a fascination on certain Catholics. They had awakened belatedly to the profound injustices of modern society, and could try to 'read off' their own situations in the light of God's 'mighty act' in delivering his people from Egypt—a frequent theme in the writings of the Latin American theologians of liberation. Marx suddenly became relevant to them. For as they transposed their biblical themes into political terms, they also found that their Christianity did not provide an analysis of society or a project for its future or a strategy for realizing that project. It may be said that it is not the function of Christianity to provide a remedy for all the ills of contemporary society—and this has frequently been stated, most recently and authoritatively in *Octogesima Adveniens* (1971). But Marxism seemed to offer all three: it has an *analysis* or explanation, a clear *project* for the future, and a *strategy*. If this suggestion is accepted as a 'working hypothesis', it would mean that Marxism does not so much replace Christianity as *supplement* it, and at the same time Christianity could revivify dogmatic, flagging Marxism by recalling its forgotten messianic origins. It would further follow that the 'protean' notion of Marxism would be still further modified in the process. The history of Marxism is not yet over.

Just as Marxism has varied and still varies, so too have the Christian responses to it. The relationship is not between one monolith and another monolith. There have been shifting patterns of response, and they will now be described. This survey of Catholic responses has two purposes. First the genetic method is the only way to understand a process which otherwise would remain deeply mysterious ('Look at the process as well as the result', advised Lord Acton). Secondly, the reader will be able to find his own place on the spectrum, for all the possible Christian attitudes, from total rejection to enthusiastic embrace, are still alive and in competition. The main problem raised by this book is still unresolved.

In the pontificate of Pope Pius XII the opposition between the Roman Catholic Church and Communism was profound, unmitigated, and constantly reinforced by acts of injustice which were countered by repeated condemnations. Even with the advantage of hindsight, it is difficult to see how it could have been otherwise at that time. A sense of *nuances* and a readiness to make distinctions were not easily found in a period in which Christians were being cast into jail and persecuted. During the 1939-45 war, the Vatican policy—or hope—was that

Communism would be defeated, but that in the process the Nazi forces would be so weakened that they would then be easily destroyed by the Allies (cf. Anthony Rhodes, *The Vatican in the Age of the Dictators*, Hodder and Stoughton, London, 1973, p. 262). Thus two dictatorships would be disposed of at a stroke. But when Russia entered the war on the Allied side, this dream was shattered, and Pope Pius XII allowed American Bishops to interpret the encyclical *Divini Redemptoris* in a more liberal sense (*ibid.*, p. 263). The Archbishop of Dubuque had not got the message and continued to make fire-eating statements. 'It is high time', he wrote, 'to stop making a distinction between the Red Army and the Soviet State. The Soviet Army is admittedly fighting heroically. But it *is* the Soviet state, as long as it is at the behest of a godless tyrant' (*ibid.*, p. 263). But once the war was over and the Red Army flooded over Europe, the need for diplomatic caution was gone. In various ways the Russians manipulated parties and parliaments, used violence and puppets, to impose their will. A trio of Cardinals— Mindszenty, Wyszinski and Beran—went to jail and symbolized resistance to this new form of tyranny. It was not a matter of the Church defending its rights or asserting its institutional privileges: the Church was defending human rights that were being monstrously trampled upon. Marxism in its Communist form had perpetrated these injustices, and it was taken as a whole: its political malpractice, its materialist philosophy, its atheism, its religious persecution, its alleged scientific claims held together and together were rejected. It was the embodiment of evil. It had confirmed in practice that it was 'intrinsically evil' as *Divini Redemptoris* had said.

Yet even within this rejection of Marxism in the cold war period, it was possible to distinguish two contrasting approaches among Christians. It could be utterly rejected, shunned as an unqualified, irredeemable evil, and identified with the Beast of the Apocalypse (cf. the intervention of Bishop Nicholas Elko, Ruthenian Bishop of Pittsburgh, at Vatican II: text in Peter Hebblethwaite, *The Council Fathers and Atheism*, Paulist Press, 1967, p. 95). Or Marxism could be considered as a phenomenon brought about by injustice in which, it was true, the 'remedy' was worse than the disease, but which would not have arisen if Christians had done their duty in line with the papal social encyclicals. The success of Communism was a symptom of a radical social disease. It spurred Christians to a form of social commitment (in Europe usually in Christian Democratic parties) in which the *aspirations* of Marxism were acknowledged to be justified but its methods and strategies were wholly rejected. Sometimes Marxism was considered as a 'Christian idea gone mad' (a Chestertonian theme developed by Berdayev, which later found its way into the encyclical *Ecclesiam Suam* of Pope Paul). The more 'progressive' Christians took the second view. And at that time the 'zeal' of Communists was often commended to Christians, and their 'cell' methods of penetration into a given *milieu* were sometimes introduced into Catholic Action. It became a frequent theme of sermons: if Communists could work so devotedly for a wrong cause, how much more eagerly should Christians give themselves to spreading the truth. The prominent British ex-Communist, Douglas Hyde, journeyed round the world developing this theme with the special authority of someone who knew from the inside how Communism worked.

Meanwhile Christians were waking up to the world in which they lived in another way which also brought them into contact with Marxists. A defensive view of the Church in which the faithful were to be protected and guarded from outside influences was proving to be unworkable. The homelands of the Christian faith, principally in the European countries which had been the historical soil of Christianity, were discovering that they were 'missionary' territories just as much as the 'foreign missions'. Unbelief had crept upon them unawares. The Church in the nineteenth century had 'lost the working classes'. Objective studies traced the sad statistical decline. The response to this situation was either to try to strengthen the defences and barricades around the dwindling minority (the 'conservative' option), or to recall to all Christians their missionary vocation (the 'progressive' view). The gift of faith was not given to be buried in the ground or hidden away in a napkin. If the Church had 'lost the workers', it must now 'go to them'. It could not rest content with waiting for them to return of their own accord. The parish was to become evangelical and missionary. These ideas found expression in the YCW movement, in the priest-workers in France, the Little Brothers of Charles de Foucauld, and many other movements that flowed into the stream that carried the Second Vatican Council. Arriving in the world of the workers, they found the Communist Party already there, and despite occasional flirtations with it, the basic strategy remained one of opposition and rivalry. Marxism was still seen chiefly as the most aggressive instance of unbelief.

Against this background one can begin to appreciate the full significance of *Pacem in Terris*, the encyclical of Pope John XXIII which was also his 'last will and testament' to a world in need of reconciliation. We now know that he had convened a small editorial committee to work on the draft of the encyclical shortly after his doctors had told him in November 1962 that he had less than a year to live (cf. Giancarlo Zizola, *L'Utopia di Papa Giovanni*, Cittadelle Editrice, Assisi, 1973). He was possessed by a great sense of urgency. The Kennedy-Khrushchev understanding after the Cuban crisis had given the world a momentary respite, but Pope John feared that it was merely a lull in the headlong arms race. He told Msgr. Pavan that he could no longer hesitate: 'I can't attribute ill-will to either side. If I do, there will be no dialogue and doors will be closed'. But the early drafts of *Pacem in Terris* met with much criticism. Fr. Ciappi, the gaunt Dominican who held the title of Master of the Sacred Palace, was alarmed by what he read, discovered an attempted synthesis with the modern thought which had been repudiated in papal teaching since the days of Gregory XVI, and detected more than a hint of liberalism and indifferentism. The Jesuit Georges Jarlot was also critical, and pointed out that the passages on collaboration between Catholics and Communists could lead to the danger of 'ideological contamination'. He warned Pope John against the danger of naively accepting 'the outstretched hand'. Other critics pointed out that elections were due in Italy on 28 April 1963, and that the Communist press would not be slow to exploit any hint of weakness.

But Pope John ignored all these objections. He did not

allow the Italian scene to dictate and distort his international policy. He enshrined in *Pacem in Terris* a series of liberating distinctions. He distinguished, first of all, between 'a false philosophy' about man and the world, and the 'economic, social and political programs' that issued from it (*Pacem in Terris*, n. 159). The 'philosophy' was false and was repudiated, but it did not exist in the abstract: it was involved in history and changing conditions. And the actual programs could, as it were, be good by accident: 'Besides, who can deny the possible existence of good and commendable elements in these programs, elements which do indeed conform to the dictates of right reason, and are an expression of man's lawful aspirations?' This was a vague enough commendation, and Pope John gave no examples of what he meant, but it was enough to break the ideological log-jam. Dialogue and cautious collaboration could begin. Pope Paul restated these principles in *Ecclesiam Suam* dated 6 August 1964 (cf. *The Council Fathers and Atheism*, Peter Hebblethwaite, Paulist Press, 1967) and the Council pointedly refrained from any renewed condemnations of Marxism or Communism. According to Zizola (p. 184) this was because a deal had been reached with the Russians: if there were no condemnations, the Russian Orthodox Observers would go to Rome for the Council. In any case 'condemnations' were foreign to the spirit of Vatican II. As Pope John said in his opening speech, the Church today 'prefers to make use of the medicine of mercy rather than that of severity. She considers that she meets the needs of the present day by demonstrating the validity of her teaching rather than by condemnations' (Abbott, p. 716). It was this last phrase that persuaded the hesitant Russians to come. The finger-wagging Church of the Syllabus of Errors gave way to the Church which sought to detect the workings of the Holy Spirit even in the most unexpected places; and the centralizing authoritarian Church which Vatican I had powerfully reinforced gave place to a more fraternal Church in which the watchwords would be discrimination and dialogue. Even with Marxists.

The new mood was accurately summed up in the title of a book by Roger Garaudy: *From Anathema to Dialogue* (French

Edition, Plon 1965; English Edition, Collins, 1967). The book was explicitly presented as an answer to Pope John's call to 'all men of good will' in *Pacem in Terris*. 'It is by no means presumptuous', wrote Garaudy, 'for a Marxist to answer in a fraternal manner the appeal fraternally addressed to all' (Preface). The moral disarmament implied here was something new. And the idea that Christians and Marxists could talk together, without exchanging insults and abuse and without aiming to convert the other side, was a novel one.

Yet it had been prophetically anticipated by Pierre Teilhard de Chardin. He had written in 1947:

Take at this very moment the two extremes around you, on the one side a Marxist, on the other a Christian, each convinced of the truth of his own particular doctrine, but both, we must suppose, inspired by an equal and radical faith in Man. Is it not certain—is it not indeed a fact of daily experience—that these two men, in so far as they believe, and in so far as they feel that the other believes strongly in the future of the world, experience for each other and as man to man a deep-seated sympathy—not just a sentimental sympathy but a sympathy based on evidence as yet dimly perceived that they are travelling on the same road, and that somehow or other and in spite of the conflict between their dogmas (*formules*) they will finish up by finding each other on the same mountain-peak? Both in their own way, no doubt, and diverging in different directions, think they have once and for all solved the ambiguity of the world. But this divergence is in reality neither complete nor final. . . . Pursued to the end the two trajectories cannot but draw together. For, of its very nature, that which is of faith, rises; and what rises must inevitably meet (*The Future of Man*, Collins, pp. 191-192).

It was the habit of Teilhard to launch his intuitions on the world without overmuch explanation or detailed justification. The Marxism he envisaged in 1947—at the height of Stalinism—owed as much to hope as to experience.

But Teilhard's surprising words did not simply echo in the void and die away. By 1960 Roger Garaudy, a member at that date of the Central Committee of the French Communist Party, had replied to the Jesuit visionary:

It is a fact that the work of Père Teilhard de Chardin opens the way for a fruitful dialogue between Christian thought and Marxism. From the very outset our dialogue with Père Teilhard has not been affected by the prejudices of a social conservatism or by any signs of distrust of science or of the sheer joy of living. It opens the way for a dialogue because of the optimistic spirit which it spreads abroad and inspires —because of his insight that the uniqueness of the human phenomenon far from excludes a historical origin of the human spirit and intelligence, because of his unconditional affirmation of the meaning of history, and because of his condemnation of the desperate individualism of the thinkers of Western decadence (*Perspectives sur l'Homme*, 1960, p. 203).

The stage was set for a dialogue in which Christians and Marxists could learn from each other.

2
Hesitations
on the Frontier

Between 1965 and 1967 the *Paulusgesellschaft*, a group of German-speaking theologians and scientists whose aim was to find a contemporary language for faith, held three successive meetings with Marxists in Salzburg, Chiemsee and Marianské Lazné (better known as Marienbad). 'A Christian-Marxist Summit Meeting', said one newspaper headline after Chiemsee, inaccurately if understandably. The meetings had no 'official' status. They were neither supported by the Communist Party nor blessed by the Church. But they were nevertheless important as the first public and international attempt of Christians and Marxists to emerge from the trenches and talk to each other in a rational way instead of exchanging slogans.

They were also the first effort to put some intellectual stiffening into the notion of 'ideological co-existence'. There was a *de facto* co-existence which came from inhabiting together a small and—in the atomic era—dangerous planet. But beyond this apprehension of a common danger, was any kind of intellectual disarmament and *rapprochement* possible? And could Christians and Marxists actually learn from each other? Even to ask such questions was anathema in some quarters, and the right-wing press predictably talked of a 'Christian capitulation' and 'loss of nerve'. But such premature judgments were not confirmed by the event.

Anyone with a sense of humor—and I can't say that none such were actually present, though they certainly lay low—must have been struck by the incongruity of the settings of these meetings. The dialogue moved from the glittering Knights' Hall in Salzburg to the island of Chiemsee in Bavaria, where the mad King Ludwig II built an extraordinary castle and dreamed Wagnerian dreams. The first meeting on Communist soil in 1967 represented a great breakthrough, but Marienbad is a spa where crumbling hotels line the streets like fading dowagers and the memory of aristocratic adulteries is still alive. These improbable settings heightened the feeling of moving somewhere in the stratosphere, out of reach of ordinary mortals. The grandiose themes confirmed the feeling. It was no doubt necessary to clear the ground with 'Ideological Co-existence' at Salzburg. But at Chiemsee the theme was 'Christian Humanity and Marxist Humanism', while 'Creativity and Freedom in a Humane Society' was discussed at Marienbad. However, these topics were in fact shrewdly chosen to link up with the inner-Marxist debate that had been going on in some Communist countries. Much could depend on a nuance, an adjective or a slight switch of emphasis. Dialogue was only possible with Marxist revisionists. 'Revisionism' is a vague rag-bag term. Its precise content varies, and is best illustrated by the examples that will be given in this chapter. It was initially a term of abuse, used by the Communist Party to describe and dismiss those who disagreed with it. It was not, therefore, a title which Marxist philosophers hastened to claim. If they gave themselves a label at all, they preferred to be called 'modern' Marxists. But 'revisionism' can be used as a neutral descriptive term to cover those Marxists who, after Stalinism, tried to rethink their Marxism.

The process began in Yugoslavia for the obvious reason that after the break with Russia in 1948, Yugoslav intellectuals felt obliged to devise a version of Marxism that could be distinguished from the standardized Russian model. They claimed that 'self-management' was the essence of Marxism. The philosophers gathered in the group called *Praxis* in Zagreb had been saying out loud what others had said only in whispers. They denounced Stalin and Stalinism because it had transformed the dictatorship of the workers into the dictatorship of the party, and then the dictatorship of the party into the dictatorship of an individual (cf., e.g., Mihailo Markovic, *Praxis*, 1/2 1969, p. 47).

They admitted that 'exploitation' and 'alienation', far from having been abolished by the Revolution, had survived in new and more damaging forms. Milovan Djilas went so far as to say that under capitalism you at least knew who was exploiting you; under socialism you simply did not know.

But the dissident Yugoslavs were out on a limb. The Polish philosophers, Adam Schaff and Leszek Kolakowski, were of more central importance. It was with them that the Marxist debate on 'humanism' really began. It was an attempt to solve the problems facing Marxism after Khrushchev's denunciation of Stalin at the Twentieth Party Congress. Khrushchev's recital of Stalin's misdeeds raised difficult problems for Communists. For now they were forced to admit facts which had long been proclaimed in the 'capitalist' press and which they had steadfastly rejected as fabrications. Overnight, the 'revered father of the people', whose outstanding genius had inspired scientific advance, victory in battle and an enormous increase in industrial output, was revealed as a monstrous tyrant. Admitting the distressing facts about the slave labour camps was one thing, but the theoretical problem they posed was even more embarrassing: Marxist ideologues had to try to explain how the corruptions of Stalinism were possible.

Were they the aberration of a demented individual, or were they attributable to the 'system' which had given birth to him? Either explanation led to further difficulties. If the personality of Stalin was to be blamed for what had happened, then the explanation was distinctly un-Marxist, since it was inconceivable in Marxist theory that an individual could single-handedly swing post-revolutionary history in so catastrophic a direction. But if, on the other hand, Stalin was a product of the system, then the system was very largely intact, and no one was showing any enthusiasm for its demolition: leaders still emerged after an invisible power struggle, the inflexible chain of command was still in place, and the Gulag Archipelago, later to be documented with such painstaking thoroughness by Alexander Solzhenitsyn, was still dealing with real and imaginary dissidents. Moreover, Khrushchev had been a party to many of the crimes which he had denounced in Stalin. He had come to power by ousting possible rivals. And the crushing of the Hungarian Revolution in 1956 meant that not all the misdeeds could be off-loaded onto Stalin and relegated to the past. Khrushchev, too, had blood on his hands, and by ordering troops into Hungary he showed that he rejected the theory that there were 'different roads to socialism'. From the point of view of the Russians, there was only one road.

The Polish philosophers, consequently, had very little room for maneuvering. They were not unfolding a doctrine in a leisurely academic manner. They were taking risks in a borderline situation. They had to keep in mind the requirements of the censors—not the best equipped of men philosophically—and so they made use of guarded understatements or retreated behind parables. Adam Schaff was not philosophizing in a vacuum when he declared that there had been 'a general undermining of criteria of judgment, a widespread crisis of values, and a feeling of insecurity about one's own fate' (*A Philosophy of Man*, Lawrence and Wishart, London, 1963, p. 70). The arbitrariness of Stalinism had not been good for anyone's nerves. Polish youth was disenchanted with Marxism and flirted with existentialism. Schaff briefly allowed himself to wonder why this should be, but he made no concessions. His own philosophy of freedom remains firmly within the guidelines of Marxist orthodoxy: 'I am free on the basis of determinism, within the framework of determinism' (*Marx oder Sartre?* Stuttgart, 1964, p. 73).

Where Schaff differed from Stalinist thinkers was in his admission that in the socialist countries, 'all the elements of Marx's analysis of alienation remain in a different form' (*Marxismus und das menschliche Individuum*, Europa Verlag, Vienna, 1965, p. 310). Alienations had not been swept away. On the contrary, modern industrial society, whether organized on capitalist or socialist lines, could lead to new forms of alienation of which Marx had not dreamed. The individual worker still felt uninvolved and uncommitted, and there was a danger that he might become the victim of an indifferent bureaucracy which transformed legitimate 'power over things' into abusive 'power over people'. This admission of the inadequacies of socialism was at odds with the clichés of propaganda which proclaimed that socialism brought the end of all alienations. Schaff's modest breach in the system opened the way to self-criticism and an honest look at 'the witness of the facts'. It left room for progress and improvement. Communism was not, said Schaff, a permanent state, arrived at in one leap after the revolution. It was rather an horizon which beckoned from afar, 'an ideal, a model, a limit towards which we strive through an unending process' (*ibid.*, p. 258). And to clinch his argument, Schaff was able to quote a forgotten text from Marx: 'Communism is not for us a stable state which is to be established, an ideal to which reality will have to adjust itself. We call communism the *real movement* which abolishes the present state of things' (Marx and Engels, *Basic Writings on Politics and Philosophy*, ed. Lewis S. Feuer, Anchor, New York, 1959, p. 257). Marxism had always been a form of this-wordly eschatology, a doctrine about the future. But in Schaff one sees the transition from the Stalinist idea that the 'future' had already arrived, and was therefore an absolute, immune to criticism, to the more modest notion that the journey towards it had begun. It was a move, in Christian language, from a 'realized eschatology' to an 'inaugurated eschatology'. Dialogue became less unthinkable.

Leszek Kolakowski made the same point. Communism, he wrote, is an horizon, 'and there is no place where this horizon exists, although every day can prepare us for it' (*Der Mensch ohne Alternative*, Piper, Munich, 1964, p. 237). Later on, in exile, Kolakowski came to denounce 'institutionalized Marxism' as pernicious. But already in the early 1960's he showed more courage than Schaff in drawing out the consequences of 'Marxist humanism' for morality and personal responsibility. Stalinist thinkers had no hesitation in declaring that all morality was class-morality, and this enabled them to designate all opponents as class enemies and crush them accordingly. No further justification was needed. Kolakowski came to reject this position as the destruction of morality, for the end cannot be used to justify the means: 'When a man is dying of hunger and you can give him something to eat, there is no combination of circumstances in which it would be right to say: "It is tactically better to allow him to die" ' (*ibid.*, p. 248). This was unusually plain speaking. More often Kolakowski cast his thought in the form of parables (later collected in *The Devil and Scripture*, Oxford University Press, 1973). In his most famous parable, *The Priest and the Jester,* he contrasted the 'bureaucrat' who values orderliness at the expense of humanity with the 'jester' who is continually critical of all authority. Though Schaff and Kolakowski were to come into conflict with each other after the 1966 celebrations of the tenth anniversary of the 'Polish Spring', at the time of the first Christian-Marxist dialogue they seemed to represent a more humanist and honest version of Marxism. They symbolized the hope of 'change from within'. Their ideas were widely canvassed abroad. They seemed more serious portents for the future than Marxist thinkers who lived comfortably and without risk in Western democratic countries.

But, ironically, Adam Schaff, philosopher of freedom, was not allowed to take part in the dialogue he had helped to prepare. At the last moment, and for unstated reasons, his passport was withheld. Nor was Kolakowski allowed out of Poland. These heavy-handed administrative measures illustrated one of the perils of the attempt at Christian-Marxist dialogue: on the Communist side, the intellectual exchanges depended entirely on Party approval and the whim of the men of power. The shadow of powerful institutions fell across the scene.

The banning of Schaff was a mistake and a self-inflicted wound. It cast doubt on the depth and sincerity of the new policy of dialogue. It undermined in advance the liberal case put forward by the Italian Communists who, at that date, had not the slightest prospect of actually exercising power. Nothing daunted, at Salzburg Lucio Lombardo-Radice stated that in the new society they wished to create, 'free expression of opinion must not only be allowed, but is necessary in order to prevent failures and to progress more rapidly. . . . The state in socialist society may not make distinctions between citizens on the basis of ideology'. Welcome news: but the complaint of Christians in Eastern Europe was precisely that Communist orthodoxy was required for any serious post, and that those who could not pass the test were second-class citizens. Lombardo-Radice knew this too, and consciously set himself in opposition to the East Europeans by suggesting that 'a Marxist takeover of the liberal idea of the confessionless state would be fruitful'. Lombardo-Radice was not alone in the Italian Communist Party which based its revisionism on the ideas of its leader, Togliatti. His Testament, which appeared posthumously in April 1964 and was even published in *Pravda*, rejected the notion of a 'centralized international organization', opposed attempts to create 'exterior uniformity', and insisted on the right of each party to develop its own policies. The Italian Communist Party has at least had the merit of consistency for over a decade.

And it has been criticized for over a decade. At Chiemsee in 1966 the Hungarian Jozsef Szigeti warned that 'the ideological neutrality of the state, or any kind of separation between Marxist politics and the Marxist world-view, cannot be made a condition of dialogue, as many today suppose.' In other words, there was no room in the Marxist concept of the state for the luxury of private options. Even Lombardo-Radice had conceded that the 'lay state', which would favor neither atheism nor religion, was a *liberal* rather than a Marxist idea. This debate is still unresolved. At the Twenty-Fifth Congress of the Russian Communist Party in March 1976, Signor Enrico Berlinguer astonished the delegates by his outspoken commitment to religious and cultural freedom. The closing words of his peroration were: 'The working-class can and must affirm an historic function within a pluralist and democratic society.' Unimpressed, Mr. Brezhnev insisted that there must be no relaxation on the ideological front.

If the Italian Communist Party was already toying with such adventurous ideas in 1965, the French Party was still as Stalinist and monolithic as ever, with the exception of Gilbert Mury and Roger Garaudy. Garaudy was to become the mainstay of these early dialogues. His isolation within the French Party foreshadowed his eventual expulsion and disgrace in 1970. He was one of the first casualties of dialogue, and in 1975 announced his conversion to a form of Christianity. But all that lay in the future, and in 1965 many considered that Garaudy had undergone a strange apprenticeship for dialogue. Through-

out the 1950's he had churned out volume after volume in which
all the twists of the Party line were faithfully defended and
explained. He had, for example, attributed Sartre's criticism of
the Russian intervention on Hungary in 1956 to 'proud individualism' and a failure of nerve, and absurdly declared that Sartre
was contributing to a climate of Fascism. Garaudy was severely
judged. David Caute said of him that for many years he had
'prowled the wide oceans of the "intellectual superstructure"
like a snub-nosed pike, biting the tails of genuine salmon, notably Sartre. . . . Humorless and without the faintest spark of
originality (Marx and Lenin have never let him down), he has
displayed that profound mediocrity of mind which is the cardinal virtue of the Stalinist and Neo-Stalinist intellectual gen-
darme' (*Collisions*, Quartet Books, London, 1974, p. 129).
George Lichteim was hardly less severe: 'Garaudy's tone was
hardly distinguishable from that of embattled party propagan-
dists such as André Stil, André Wurmser, *et autres Kanapas*'
(*Marxism in Modern France*, Columbia University Press, 1966,
p. 108).

But these harsh judgments, accurate enough for the 1950's,
are misleading because they freeze and harden one period in
Garaudy's life. They neglect the possibility of conversion and
metanoia. The revelations about Stalin's brutal tyranny produced a delayed-action shock and eventually, when they sank in,
a sense of guilt. By the 1960's Garaudy had changed. One of the
values he discovered in Christianity was precisely its stress on
the need to 'turn back' and 'start again', on the need for conversion and perpetual reconversion. It was not a religion of fata-
lism or passivity. This simple insight led him to reformulate the
'Marxist attitude to religion'. Garaudy claimed that there were
two ways of thinking of religion in Marx. It could be regarded
as an illusion, 'opium for the people', which provided a distrac-
tion from urgent tasks here below by offering the mirage of a
heaven hereafter. But there was another strand in Marxism,
said Garaudy, which held that religion could be regarded as 'the
expression of real distress and the protest against real distress'
(Marx in *Contribution to the Critique of Hegel's Philosophy
of Right*, Moscow, p. 42). This was a crucial distinction. For

it meant that religion could not simply be judged *a priori* and dismissed in advance as necessarily reactionary. One would have to see how it behaved in precise situations to determine whether it turned people towards or away from the world. Marx's emphasis on religion as an 'alienation' could be explained by his youthful experience of the German Pietistic tradition which tended to be passive and highly conservative, a mere consecration of the political *status quo*. But in the twentieth century, Garaudy maintained, the Second Vatican Council had encouraged a set of new attitudes which answered the charge of alienation: religion could inspire a *protest* against real distress, and a protest which led to action. With this distinction between religion as alienation and religion as protest, Garaudy hoped to achieve two results. He wanted to encourage Christians to 'join in the revolutionary movement', and at the same time to forestall and disarm the Christian objection to the systematic atheism and hostility to religion which had characterized Marxism in its Communist form. He succeeded to the extent that the distinction has subsequently been regarded by the Christian Left as self-evident.

But Garaudy insisted that dialogue did not involve either 'compromise or eclecticism'. It was rather a kind of mutual emulation process, as a result of which 'your faith should be purer and our Marxism richer and more critical'. It would lead not only to a better understanding of the other side, when the straw men and caricatures of controversy were set aside, but to a better understanding of one's own positions. For it is one thing to expound Christian faith to an already committed audience, and quite another to try to state it in the presence of critical opponents. This is a valuable exercise in stripping down to essentials. But could one go further and suggest that Christianity and Marxism could positively learn from each other? And what, in the concrete, was to be learned?

Marxists could learn from Christianity about man's deepest aspirations, about what they technically called 'subjectivity'. That men should conceive of a Christ whose love is infinite is a 'beautiful idea', and this act of faith 'proves that man never considers himself wholly defeated' *(From Anathema to*

Dialogue, Herder and Herder, New York, 1966 / Collins, London, 1967, p. 75). For Garaudy, Marxists needed Christianity to save them from one-dimensional triviality: 'Marxism would be the poorer if St. Paul and St. Augustine, St. Theresa of Avila, Pascal and Claudel, and the Christian meaning of the transcendence of love were to become foreign to it' (*ibid.*, p. 77). At this stage of his development, Garaudy's underlying thought was that Christianity provided a symbolic language to express deep human aspirations. The greatness of religion was that it asked permanently valid questions; its weakness was that it rushed in to answer them too soon and too dogmatically. The task of Marxism was 'to rediscover, beneath the myths, the aspirations which brought them forth' (*ibid.*, p. 78). What Christians, meanwhile, were supposed to learn from Marxism, was stated rather more clearly: they could learn the inadequacy of discourse about 'ends' which did not discuss the means of their realization. It had to be conceded that much uplifting Christian talk about 'the dignity of man' and 'the love of one's neighbor' unfortunately omitted to say how these noble ideas were to be put into practice. There could be a flagrant contradiction between ideals and life. Marxism, claimed Garaudy, had taught Christians to commit themselves politically in order to realize the ideals of the Gospel, and so Christianity was ceasing to be, in Nietzsche's contemptuous phrase, 'a Platonism for the masses'.

For all its amiability and sympathy, Garaudy's interpretation of Christianity stopped short of respecting its uniqueness. Christianity was understood as a collection of myths which revealed deep human aspirations. In Garaudy's scenario—and he was later followed by many others, notably Vitězslav Gardavsky—the Marxist student of Christianity acts as a kind of therapist: he listens keenly to the Christian, nodding empathetically from time to time to encourage his patient, but he is really on the lookout for 'the hidden agenda', for the 'story behind the story'. This therapeutic listening technique may be traced back to Marx himself. He is commonly said to have 'turned Hegel upside down': one could also say that he had reinterpreted Hegel's metaphysics as mystified economics (cf. Neil

McInnes, *The Western Marxists*, Alcove Press 1962, p. 16). It was, moreover, inevitable that Marxism should have this reductive attitude to Christianity, so long as it retained its claim to embody the meaning of history. As late as 1970, Garaudy continued to explain that Marxism was 'not one among a number of philosophies but an awareness of the underlying movement that governs our history, the Promethean enterprise of taking control of the process of development and of deliberately building up the future' (*Marxism in the Twentieth Century*, Collins, 1970, p. 9). Even if we leave Prometheus aside as a rhetorical flourish, the claim to possess the key to contemporary history meant that, at best, Christianity could throw light only on man's muddled aspirations to brotherhood and justice. It could illumine the private area of 'subjectivity', but not the tough real world of class-conflict.

However, it is fair to add that some Christians responded to Marxism by trying to assimilate it in an exactly parallel way. Although Karl Rahner had begun to speak of 'anonymous Christians' some years before the Christian-Marxist dialogue began, this theory provided him with a framework into which the 'implicity Christian' values of Marxism could be fitted. In an essay called 'On the Possibility of Christian Faith Today' he wrote:

> I see thousands around me—I see whole cultures, whole epochs of history around me, before and after me—who are not explicitly Christian. I see the approach of times in which Christianity will no longer be a matter of course in Europe and in the whole world. I know all that, but ultimately it cannot really trouble me. Why not? Because I see everywhere a *nameless Christianity*, and because I do not see my own explicit Christianity as one option *among* others which contradict it. I see nothing other in my Christianity than the explicit recognition and home-coming of everything in the way of truth and love which exists or could exist anywhere else (*Theological Investigations*, 5, Darton, Longman and Todd, London, 1966, p. 9).

Where Marxism shows a concern for truth and love, for genuine brotherhood and human solidarity, then these real values must be traced back ultimately to their source in the grace of Christ. Marxists could turn out to be 'anonymously Christian'. Since most people resent being told that they are *really* 'something other' than what they explicitly claim to be, there was no question of lecturing Marxists or informing them of their new and rather surprising status. Yet this theory was in the background of the dialogue. When two absolutist systems meet, neither will be content until it has encompassed, explained, and to some extent 'recovered' the other. This was verified in the dialogues of the 1960's.

Garaudy's revisionism had its limits. He continued to affirm that Communism would bring a definitive breakthrough in human history. 'Authentically human history', he declared in Salzburg, 'will begin with Communism. It will be a history which is no longer made up of class-struggle and war' (*From Anathema to Dialogue*, p. 79). Little attempt was made to check this statement against the actual experience of Communist countries. Russian ideologues tried to account for the gap between theory and practice by saying that selfish tendencies inherited from capitalism delayed the emergence of the new socialist man. More than half a century after the Revolution of 1917, this seemed rather a lame argument. Garaudy was equally theoretical: Communism, he explained, is not 'the end of history' *tout court*: it is merely the end of 'pre-history' (*ibid.*, p. 79). Obscure, irritating and unverifiable as such statements were, they at least had the merit of making clear how crucially important is the question of eschatology in Marxism. Moreover, there was a clear link between such theoretical affirmations and the totalitarian forms of Marxism which actually existed. For if the end of 'history' or even merely of 'pre-history' has been announced, there seems to be no room for alternative views of society, and a regime based on this presumptuous claim can be imposed on people who have not freely consented to it in the name of a deeper insight into the 'laws of history'.

In Salzburg Karl Rahner attacked this vulnerable point. He made a clear distinction between Christian 'hope' and Marxist 'Utopianism'. Christian eschatology is not a this-worldly utopia, and the Kingdom of God cannot be reduced to the classless society. However, the two visions of the future are not contradictory, since they are not on the same level, and they can be related to each other in so far as the Christian doctrine of hope 'fills the vacuum left by the Marxist expectation for the future'. Marxism arouses a craving which it cannot satisfy. Moreover, continued Rahner, it is highly dangerous to turn the future into an idol on whose altar present generations can be sacrificed; and it is illusory to attempt to fix and freeze permanently a particular state of society, 'after the revolution', and to declare that it embodies the absolute. This was the context in which Rahner developed the idea of God as 'the Absolute Future', in whose light every human society without exception will be open to criticism (cf. *Theological Investigations*, 6, pp. 58-68). The function of God, to use the language of sociology, is to prevent the divinization of anything less than God, whether it be the state or the party or the future.

Rahner returned to these themes at Chiemsee a year later. Although he conceded that a Christian humanism, based on the Incarnation, could be developed, he insisted that the Christian theologian must put a question mark against every form of humanism. Death is the awkward fact that no finesse of dialectic can spirit away. It relativizes all humanisms, for it is the moment when we accept the mystery of the God whom we cannot manipulate or mold according to our desires. And death likewise relativizes every form of civilization and social organization, including the Marxist project. Christians can collaborate in the building up of a more just society, but they will never make the mistake of absolutizing any one form of society. The past will be no guide to the future. But one condition must be rigorously maintained in all attempts to 'build the future': 'Right order (*das Recht*) can exist only where those in power are prepared to limit themselves in its exercise, because man is only truly human when he abandons the claim to be an absolute and asserts firmly the pluralism of the world, however great the drive towards unity'. Finally, Rahner had no doubt that religion would survive in Communist societies simply because the fundamental questions which it asks about the value of the individual and the meaning of life can never be suppressed. Energetic persecution, systematic indoctrination, and complete state control of the mass media would not be enough to root them out, because they are a part of what it means to be human.

Abstract though Rahner's treatment of Marxism might seem, it touched on some raw nerves and linked up with the discussions which had been going on among revisionist Marxists. Schaff and Kolakowski, by presenting Communism as a receding and inaccessible horizon, had introduced into it an element of relativity. They postponed the great eschatological day. Meanwhile, Czechs like Milan Machovec̆ were agonizing over the abuses of power within Marxism, and finding discreet understatements with which to express their worry: 'Precisely because power was used so thoughtlessly in the Marxist movement, and indeed abused, so that thousands of honest men have suffered, many Marxists began to wonder whether there was not a deeper and more legitimate interpretation of force and its limits than had hitherto been in use' (*A Marxist Looks at Jesus*, Darton, Longman and Todd, 1976, p. 33). Another Czech philosopher, Vit̆ezslav Gardavsky, attempted to explain away the absolutization of the state in Stalinism. 'We should not be surprised', he charitably wrote, 'if, in the eyes of those who have made the sacrifice, Communism has taken on the form of an absolute goal, compared to which everything else, even they themselves, has become a mere means to an end' (*God Is Not Yet Dead*, Penguin, 1973, p. 207). He went on to reject this position, but in the name of the cloud-cuckoo notion of 'the open future'. More generally, many Marxists believed that in denouncing Stalinism they were rejecting the arbitrary exercise of power and the idolization of the state. Marxism was to be rescued from Stalinism. These examples show that Marxists, too, could ask the questions posed by Karl Rahner. But that is not enough to dispose of his *critique* of Marxism, for the simple reason that institutional Marxism never shared any of these doubts and that all the writers mentioned in this paragraph could be dismissed as 'revisionist'. They were out of the mainstream. They were heretics who had no power to change the situation. They spoke only for themselves.

But none of this was self-evident in 1967, when the Paulus-gesellschaft met for the first time in a Communist country. It seemed not unreasonable to hope that Marxism, once it had exorcised the bad dream of Stalinism, would find the resources within its own tradition that would enable it to move towards a form of society in which the people had a voice and human rights were respected. At Marienbad in 1967 the 'revisionists' were in the ascendent. In any other context, their remarks would have been truisms, but in Novotny's Czechoslovakia they were explosive. 'Science', declared Dr. Josef Macek at the opening session, 'is international', and he explained that just as science today refuses to be the handmaid of theology, so also it refuses to be the handmaid of ideology. Having proclaimed the autonomy of science, he placed his head on the block by adding, 'We are here to test our systems against reality'. Stalinist thinkers were content to establish the truth by metaphysical proclamation, and prudently refrained from bourgeois notions of verification.

Dr. Milan Pruha, a philosopher who had studied in Moscow and Paris, widened the gap opened up by Macek. He made a plea for pluralism in Marxist philosophical work. As a matter of intellectual honesty, Marxist philosophers would have to tackle Wittgenstein, Husserl, Heidegger, Merleau-Ponty and Teilhard de Chardin, and these authors could not be dismissed in advance as utterly misguided. Pruha sketched out a philosophy of 'being' that would have made sense to a disciple of Heidegger if not to a follower of Aquinas. Cesare Luporini, Professor of Philosophy in Florence, interrupted to point out that to make 'being' the key concept of philosophy is to produce 'a speculative transposition of Marxism'. Marx always began from the analysis of actual societies. But Pruha coolly replied that if one confines oneself to the analysis of society, one *ipso facto* excludes a whole range of philosophical problems which have been raised and cannot be ignored. He did not propose to ignore them. He believed that philosophy was a 'living organism' and that it was dangerous to absolutize any one point of view. 'Revisionism' could hardly be pushed any further.

The 'revisionists' received support and encouragement

from the Christian side in the contributions of Giulio Girardi. His knowledge of Marxism was more direct and intimate than that of Rahner, and he had 'cleared' his Chiemsee speech with members of the Italian Communist Party. They approved it because, instead of criticism from the outside, it provided a basis for an 'alternative' version of Marxism from within. Girardi analyzed what he called Marxist 'integrism' or rigid, dogmatic Marxism. It operated with the aid of a series of antinomies—base and superstructure, class and humanity, institution and person, history and the individual, and on each level subordinated and sometimes sacrificed the individual human person to the state or the party or history. And this was the version of Marxism that officially prevailed in Eastern Europe. It reduced 'man' to 'economic man'. However, this Marxist 'integrism' could be overcome by a return to the 'young' Marx, whose concept of 'liberation' (significant term for the future) implied considerably more than economic progress and the redistribution of wealth: it implied also cultural and social values. At Chiemsee, Girardi issued an invitation: 'A regime which the people did not freely accept would not be a truly Marxist regime. Marxism should run the risk of liberty. . . . The time has come to offer to an adult humanity an adult form of Marxism'.

At Marienbad in 1967, Girardi's questions became more insistent still. One can grant, he said, that the road from socialism to communism is more winding and more rugged than Marx had supposed; but is it necessary systematically to prolong the intermediate stage of collectivization and state ownership, in which power is concentrated in the hands of a few and which perpetuates the state of alienation the revolution set out to abolish? Luciano Gruppi immediately retorted that one could not describe the socialist states in these terms and claimed that they had great popular support. In that case, said Girardi, you need not hesitate to move towards participation in decision-making, and everything possible should be done to bring about this 'qualitative leap'. 'Our objection', said Girardi, 'is not that our Marxist friends are revolutionary, but that they are not revolutionary enough, and that a revolution begun in the name of freedom should not have been carried through to its conclusion'. Girardi's whole effort was directed towards ridding Marxism of

the burden of Stalinism. He tried to bring about a radical
change among Marxists by holding up to them a vision, based
on their own sources, of a renewed and revivified Marxism. He
stated the options with great clarity: 'There is a Marxism that is
open to dialogue, the Marxism of men. And there is a Marxism
that is closed to dialogue, the Marxism of institutions. Our
hope, and the hope of the world, is that in this dramatic tension
between man and institution, the final victory will belong to
man' (*Marxism and Christianity*, Gill, Dublin, 1968, p. 204).

But there was a third Christian response to Marxist revisionism that was midway between Rahner's philosophical rejection and Girardi's conditional embrace. It was illustrated by
Johannes Baptist Metz. Metz accepted Marxism as a challenge
that could stimulate Christians to abandon political indiffer-
ence, individualism and what he called 'the privatization of
hope'. Christians are defined most simply in the New Testament
as 'men who have hope' (1 Thess. 4, 13) and Metz built his
'political theology' on Christian hope. The Church hopes not
merely for itself, but for all men, since it is 'the sacrament of
hope for all mankind'. Moreover, Christian hope cannot be
merely a patient and passive waiting for the fruits of a victory
that has already been won in principle. It implies a commitment
to change in the present. This life cannot be reduced simply to a
'vale of tears' or an ante-chamber to the future life. Metz's theology had been worked out in dialogue with the East German
Marxist, Ernst Bloch, who had picturesquely declared that
Christian hope means 'not only having something to eat and
drink, but having to help with the cooking'. Or as Metz put it:
'We are builders—not merely interpreters—of a future of which
God himself is the dynamism'. Metz's theology of hope im-
pelled Christians to political commitment, and at the same time
it equipped them with the criteria of greater justice and greater
fraternity by which all societies, capitalist and socialist, could be
judged. The Kingdom always lay beyond any of its partial and
inadequate realizations. He agreed with Rahner that any claim
that the definitive form of society had already arrived was abusive, and envisaged the Church as 'an institution for the creative
criticism of society'.

Within a year of the Marienbad meeting, Novotny was

replaced by Alexander Dubcek as first secretary of the Czech
Communist Party. It would be absurd to try to establish any
direct causal link between the two events; but it would be equally hard to deny that Dubcek's 'Socialism with a human face'
would have been impossible without some intellectual preparation in depth. It did not spring from nowhere. Marienbad contributed to and was a symptom of the intellectual process. Dubcek's achievement was to provide the framework for a form of
'Western' Marxism which owed as much to the inter-war democratic tradition in Czechoslovakia as it did to Russian models. It
put some content into Togliatti's concept of 'different roads to
socialism'. Tolerance was built into the movement, and it was
extended to the Church. The mood in Prague was one of relief.
It was as though the Communist Party had ceased to be a sec-
tarian group and had become the mobilization of the nation in
its political aspect. There was intense debate about the future
course of the country as, for the first time in thirty years, people
felt at last free to speak their minds. Leading members of the
Party had the unusual experience of being challenged on television. Dubcek answered questions with rare honesty and was
genuinely popular. However, one would miss the whole point of
the events of the spring of 1968, and share the Russian view of
them, if one thought of the Czechs as exchanging Marxism for
Western liberalism. Though they were ready to learn from the
experience of others, 'Socialism with a human face' was a
development within Marxism. It illustrated the validity of
Girardi's distinction between the dogmatic Marxism of institutions and the personalist 'Marxism of men'.

But revisionism expired as the tanks rattled into Prague in
August 1968. The Marxism of institutions prevailed. Defeated
and humiliated, the 'Marxism of men' became a tragic symbol
of a might-have-been. Its advocates were one by one driven out
of public life and academic work. Defined from above and de-
cried as heretical, revisionism was condemned to lapse into a
private speculation or an underground movement. In her account of the Marienbad meeting, Dr. Erika Kadlecova, who was
to become the minister responsible for religious affairs in the
Dubcek government, predicted that the Christian-Marxist dia-

logue would run into difficulties connected with 'the vested interests of power' and 'the inner discipline of the institutions with which we are identified'. The prediction was accurate, and Dr. Kadlecova's remarks acquired a tragic ring. 'There were many complaints', she wrote, 'about the powerlessness of intellectuals who can make fine speeches but have no power to put them into effect. That is both true and false. Of course they do not have armies and prisons, and they can neither make promises nor pronounce bans. But they can create a spiritual atmosphere in which change becomes possible' ('Die Gespräche in Marienbad', in *Dialog*, 1, 1968, pp. 101-109). Those who had armies and prisons intervened. Dr. Kadlecova was removed from her post in September 1969.

The visible results of the new 'spiritual atmosphere' were meagre. Dr. Milan Machoveč, still a committed Marxist, studied the life of Jesus and wrestled with the 'disappointments' of official Marxism (*A Marxist Looks at Jesus*, Darton, Longman and Todd, 1976, 1st German edition 1972). The early Marxists were visionaries and idealists, but after 'fifty years of socialism' there is much disillusionment. Machoveč compares this process with the gradual fading of the expectation of the imminent end of the world among the early Christians: premonitions of the immediate eschatological end of all things gave way to a long-term hope, and attitudes to life, the world and marriage were changed. In a similar way, the early Marxists were enchanted by the prospect of a 'leap into the realm of freedom' and a vision of the 'radically different society' that the revolution would bring. But now Marxists feel less confident. There is no leap, only a timid and uncertain step forward.

This led Machoveč to reopen the New Testament. He discovered that many of its themes applied directly to the situation 'after fifty years of socialism'. 'Who is my neighbor?' became an urgent question in a world which had abolished 'charity' and left all forms of social care to the state. Jesus' denunciation of Pharisaism took on a new relevance in a world in which a small group of men feel convinced that 'they are not as other men are' (Lk. 18, 11) and use power for their own advantage. The abuse of power worried Machoveč most of all. Force may be, as Marx

said, the midwife of history, but it has produced many mon-
strosities. Machoveč criticizes 'the failure to distinguish clearly,
unambiguously, and indisputably between Marxist power and
criminal power' (*ibid.*, p. 33). But he has no suggestions about
how this distinction is to be upheld in practice, and in the end
seems to resign himself to 'carrying his cross daily' and recog-
nizing that, for a Marxist, there will be many situations in
which 'he must suffer injustice rather than contribute to it'
(*ibid.*, p. 34). At this point, says Machoveč, the Marxist is on
the threshold of the New Testament. Though he continues to
offer the usual Marxist socio-economic explanation for the origins of Christianity and is not on the point of conversion, it
should be clear that Machoveč's humanistic Marxism has many
of the characteristics of religious faith, not to mention hope and
charity.

But an individual case, though it may be a portent for the
future, proves nothing. Roger Garaudy, too, found himself cor-
nered. He had always insisted that the Christian-Marxist dialogue would fail if it were confined to non-representative individuals: 'The threshold will only really be crossed when
meetings will take place not between a few isolated pioneers, who
may be suspect in their own communities, but between the two
communities themselves'. Or, as he put it more succinctly: *Je ne
veux pas être d'avant garde.* But it was precisely this aspect of
Garaudy's approach to dialogue which roused the wrath of the
French Communist Party. Garaudy was attacked for underes-
timating the ideological conflict between the Church and the
Party. Antoine Casanova wrote: 'It is scientifically mistaken
and politically dangerous to put on the same level the community represented by the Party—a community which excludes and
combats class enemies—and the Catholic Church which includes all the contradictions of class-ridden society' (in *France
Nouvelle*, 8 June 1966). Garaudy's critics prevailed. At the
Party Congress in the Palais des Sports at Nanterre, in February 1970, he was expelled from the Communist Party. His last
mistake had been to publish an article in which he was invited
to answer the question: What does Christ mean for you?
Garaudy had written:

Sometime in the reign of Tiberius (*sic*), no one knows exactly where or when, a man appeared who opened a breach in the closed horizon of humanity. He was neither a philosopher nor a ruler, but he lived in such a way that his whole life proclaimed: each one of us can, at any moment, begin a future that is new. . . . (*Evangile aujourd'hui*, December 1969).

The 'Marxism of institutions' was not ready for such a novelty. It was incapable of dialogue. As Kolakowski had pointed out as long ago as 1957, where Communism is in power, 'the concept of Marxism comes to have an *institutional* and not an *intellectual* content'. From this point of view, he added, it little matters what the actual content of Marxism is alleged to be, since 'being a Marxist' simply means being ready to accept what the authorities prescribe (*Der Mensch ohne Alternative*, p. 8).

The results on the Christian side of the Christian-Marxist dialogues of the 1960's can be more briefly told. Rahner's critique of the unchecked power of official Marxism seemed to be confirmed by the events of Czechoslovakia. Metz's attempt to rival Marxism by developing an alternative 'political theology' that would provide the basis for Christian commitment in the world, when translated, had many followers who worked it out in terms of their own local situations. His systematic rejection of all political ideologies was reflected in *Octogesima Adveniens* of 1971. Finally, Girardi, who had presented a more sympathetic and humanist version of Marxism, based on the works of the young Marx, overcame the disappointment of Czechoslovakia by turning increasingly to Latin America. The record of the Christian-Marxist dialogues of the 1960's provides no evidence of convergence between the two sides, still less of any 'infiltration' of the Church by Marxism. 'Dialogue', as Albert Camus had remarked, 'is only possible between people who remain what they are and speak the truth'. Whatever happened subsequently, at this stage, dialogue contributed to a clearer awareness of identity and difference.

3
The Theologies
of Liberation

The next phase of the Christian-Marxist encounter took place in Latin America. There was a change of scene, of *dramatis personae*, of themes and of style. This was inevitable, since Latin America was 'different': it is a continent in which a form of popular Christianity has held sway—an estimated 90% of the 300,000,000 population are baptized, and baptism is an essential social requirement for rich and poor. No one need lack *padrones* in the 'continent of the godfathers'. Though often superficial and 'sociological', this residual or potential Christianity was not negligible. Could it, then, be tapped to animate and sustain radical social change throughout the continent? And could this happen without the aid of Marxists who brought their own characteristic analysis to the situation? Or, again, were not both Christians and Marxists doomed to fail unless they collaborated? And could they co-operate without compromise? The remark of Che Guevara echoed round the continent: 'When Christians have the courage to commit themselves completely to the Latin American revolution, the Latin American revolution will be invincible.'

Seen from Latin America, the dialogues described in the last chapter seemed like abstract and academic debates which were irrelevant to the huge practical problems the continent had to face. Gustavo Gutiérrez relegated them to a brief footnote, and instead of the European type of dialogue called for 'grass-roots experiments in social praxis', and said that Latin America could be regarded as a vast laboratory of social change (*A Theology of Liberation*, Orbis, 1973, p. 18, fn. 32). In a laboratory one learns to expect the unexpected, and there will be many sudden shifts of direction and frequent false trails. The real work goes on in obscurity. The 'theologies of liberation', articulated piece-meal not only in books but in hundreds of duplicated and privately circulated papers, are the fragmentary records of these still unfinished experiments.

The plural, 'theologies of liberation', is important. Marcel Niedergang wrote a book called *The Twenty Latin Americas* (The Pelican Latin American Library, 2 vols.). And since the starting point for the theologians of liberation is their own particular sociological situation, it will not do to treat Latin America as though it were a single undifferentiated blur on the map. Distinctions have to be kept in mind. A few basic facts will be enough to illustrate the problems of comparability. Argentina has hundreds of miles of common frontier with Bolivia; but whereas the population of Argentina is 100% European, Bolivia has a 60% native population and 35% are half-castes; Argentina has an illiteracy rate of only 8%, while that of Bolivia is 85%; the *per capita* income of Argentinians is eight times that of Bolivians. Again, Chile and Peru have a common frontier, but Chile's population is 96% European and the illiteracy rate is 9%; Peru is made up of 35% of Indians, 35% of half-castes, and the rest are white; moreover, 65% of the population is illiterate. And I have not mentioned Brazil, which is almost a continent to itself.

Yet despite these and many other differences, which are also reflected in the social, political and religious situations of the twenty-seven countries, it still makes sense to speak of a 'Latin American theology' with discernible common features; and it is possible to read the theologians of liberation without being particularly made aware of their countries of origin. Despite their claims to rootedness, they are not reluctant to generalize. The most influential have come from Peru (Gustavo Gutiérrez), Uruguay (Juan Segundo, S.J.), Colombia (Camilo Torres), Brazil (Joseph Comblin, Rubem A. Alves, José Míguez Bonino, Hugo Assmann) and Chile (Segundo Galilea, Gonzalo Arroyo, S.J.).

What they have in common is more important than what

divides them. They share the view that theology involves not only the understanding of faith but also a political commitment to change society. Theology is not just something that goes on in the head. It is not a theology *about* liberation; it is a theology *for* liberation. It claims to rescue theology from the effete abstractions of Western theologians. It draws freely upon Marxism. It does not mind if it disturbs the comfortable. 'It is a barbarians' theology', writes Enrique Dussel, which shocks and scandalizes the 'wise according to this world' (*Concilium*, June 1974, p. 56). Even those Western theologians who have tried to develop a 'political theology' are dismissed as 'theologians of affluence' who simply write endless prologomena to an action that never takes place. As Hugo Assmann puts in, in a metaphor of considerable confusion: 'The theology of affluence has created a sea of calm around itself, in which it can sit back and flirt at a distance with the idea of revolution, but without getting its hands dirty in the process' (*Practical Theology of Revolution*, p. 120).

These are deliberately hard sayings, and if the Western reader wants to understand, he clearly has to rise from the safe armchair of affluence and try to feel the emotional impact made by the theologians of liberation who are haunted and obsessed by the injustices of their continent. They can think of nothing else, and so can appear thoroughly unreasonable. While many Western theologians were briefly toying with 'death-of-God' theologies, the theology of liberation embodied the great hope that Christians would finally break with irrelevance and speak to the condition of the humiliated peoples of Latin America. Their existential starting point was not an idea, but an act of solidarity with the poor. Gutiérrez explains: 'If I make myself the neighbour of the man I seek out in the streets and squares, in factories and marginal *barrios*, in the fields and the mines, my world changes. This is what happens when an authentic and effective "option for the poor" is made; because, for the Gospel, the poor man is the neighbor *par excellence*. . . . But the poor do not exist as an act of destiny; their existence is not politically neutral or ethnically innocent' (*Concilium*, June 1974, p. 59).

Only when the sustaining emotional power of the movement has been understood can one grasp how men like Camilo Torres and Nestor Paz Zamora could become cult-figures and symbols of hope, and also how a form of Marxism could be so speedily accepted. Torres had based his position on the requirements of Christian humanism: 'If the good of all mankind cannot be achieved except by changing the temporal structures of society, it would be sinful for Christians to oppose change' (John Gerassi, ed., *Revolutionary Priest: The Complete Writings and Messages of Camilo Torres*, Random House, New York, 1971, p. 313). Along the path of change he found Marxists, and the over-riding need to combat established injustice enabled him to overcome without strain or contortions the anti-Communism which had dominated the Latin American Church in the previous two decades. Torres declared: 'I have said that as a Colombian, as a sociologist, as a Christian and as a priest I am a revolutionary. I believe that the Communist Party consists of truly revolutionary elements, and hence I cannot be anti-Communist either as a Colombian, a sociologist, a Christian or a priest' (*ibid.*, p. 370). Torres' revolutionary option led to his death at the hands of a Colombian army patrol in 1966.

Nestor Paz Zamora became another member of this late twentieth century martyrology. He was one of a group of seventy-five students who left La Paz University, Bolivia, to join the Teoponte guerrilla campaign in 1970. He had read Marx and pledged himself to the revolution before a picture of Che Guevara, but he also carried the Psalms and the New Testament in his kit-bag. He never came back. The Rector of La Paz University, a Marxist, honoured him with this significant tribute: 'There is a truth which hammers at our conscience; a certain Christian refused to ignore Marxists. As a result, Teoponte refused to ignore believers'. The common ground was the need for 'liberation'.

'Liberation', in the sense it is used here, is a word with a history. It grew out of the failure of the idea of 'development', the code-word of the early 1960s. The 1960s were hailed as 'the Decade of Development', President Kennedy launched his Alliance for Progress, while in *Populorum Progressio* of 1967 Pope Paul spoke of 'development as the new name for peace'. But to be declared 'underdeveloped', or more subtly in de Gaulle's phrase, *en voie de développement,* brought little comfort to the countries of Central and Latin America. On the contrary it dramatically highlighted their state of dependence on world markets, their secondary and subsidiary role in the system of international exchange. They discovered that they were the victims of economic colonialism. Seen in this light, the problems of deprivation which all these countries knew in one form or another—from the fruit-growers to the inhabitants of the *barrios* or shanty-towns—took on a different aspect. Invited to prepare a background paper for a SODEPAX consultation held at Cartigny, Switzerland, in November 1969, Gustavo Gutiérrez traced the stages which the notion of 'development' had undergone: starting life in the capitalist world as a synonym for economic growth, it had been broadened to mean 'an overall social process which included social, political and cultural aspects'. *Populorum Progressio* makes use of this wider concept of integral development.

But already the word had taken on a pejorative sense in Latin America. Gutiérrez rejected 'development' because it had come to mean reformism and modernization, a mere tinkering with the works, which did not begin to touch the inter-locking international system of trade which, on this analysis, was permanently weighted against the poorer countries. Development was a subtler way of maintaining the *status quo*—and expecting people to be grateful for it (*In Search of a Theology of Development,* A SODEPAX Report, pp. 121 *et seq.*). In the 1970's still stronger language was used. Hugo Assmann says bluntly that 'development' was a lie. The programs intended to implement it fell under 'imperialist' control. They were accompanied by the growing militarization of the continent and the setting up of powerful repressive governments with the active and sometimes overt support of the CIA (*Practical Theology of Liberation,* Search Press, London 1975, p. 49). In Brazil and Uruguay, and later in Chile, torture became part of the routine of administration. In such circumstances, development was discredited and became unusable.

'Liberation', on the other hand, expressed the determination of oppressed peoples to take their destiny into their own hands, to become the 'subject' and no longer the passive 'object' of history, and so to shake off their oppressors. Moreover, the biblical sources were beginning to be interpreted in a new way. Meeting at Medellín in September 1968, the Latin American Bishops expressed salvation in terms of *liberación* and made it their central concept. 'God has sent his Son', they declared, 'so that in the flesh he may come to liberate all men from slavery which holds them subject, from sin, ignorance, hunger, misery, oppression—in a word, from the injustice and hate which stem from human egoism'. This ringing assertion was accompanied by a defiant statement of pride in their continent: 'We have faith in God, in man, and in the values and future of Latin America'. The implication was that they would no longer be dependent on the finance and the theology of North America and Europe. By their stress on *liberación*, the Latin American Bishops gave their blessing to a movement that was already under way; and it has frequently been remarked that Medellín was for Latin America what the Council was for the rest of the Church.

In their account of liberation, the Bishops tried to maintain a balance between religious and political language. Though they shared and gave expression to the aspirations of their continent and denounced the built-in structural injustices of their societies, in their diagnosis the ultimate reason for oppression was sin and human egoism. This was the point at which most theologians of liberation began to part company with the Bishops. Medellín was merely a staging-post along the road to frankly political liberation. Its chief defect was said to be the lack of any serious analysis of the structural causes of oppression in Latin America. The theology of liberation was to remedy this defect by the use of a Marxist analysis. The Bishops had not created the movement but they provided it with legitimating cover, and, once started, it developed under its own impetus. Hugo Assmann has described the process by which episcopal documents promised more than they could deliver: 'Issued with the highest official sanction, they propose measures which are in fact beyond the capabilities of the Bishops. The Bishops, therefore, cannot adopt them, but they become a rallying-point for the *avant-garde*, which in turn prods the consciences of the hierarchies. . . ." (*Practical Theology of Liberation*, p. 135). And so on. The leftward drift became inevitable. One cannot use words like 'liberation' lightly: the words come back and point an accusing finger.

More immediately, 'liberation' implied a threefold task. First came the sociological analysis, borrowed from Marxism, which was designed to uncover the various levels of exploitation and unmask the oppressors. Next came the educational task of making the exploited *aware* of what was happening to them, and in this enterprise Paulo Freire's 'conscientization' or 'consciousness-raising' played a crucial role: it was one thing to teach an illiterate to read, but if at the same time he became aware of the remote forces which had previously kept him illiterate, then great progress was made. And finally came the struggle (*lucha*) against the oligarchies who were in alliance with the oppressors. The struggle could take various forms, according to circumstances, and there has been much intense debate about which form was appropriate. It ranged from overt political activity, where permitted, to the formation of small groups (*comunidades de base*). It could take the form of armed resistance or it could be a matter of bearing witness. But whatever form the struggle takes, struggle there must be, for neutrality is impossible. The question for theologians is no longer 'What is to be believed?' but 'What is to be done?'

Hence the theologians of liberation speak insistently of 'the primacy of action'. This emphasis is in conscious opposition to 'the primacy of the spiritual', the title of a work by Jacques Maritain, which is thought to reveal an 'idealistic' attitude. In stressing 'the primacy of action', they are not merely saying that truth must be concretely applied, nor simply that truth is tested or verified in its application. They are saying that truth *does not exist* except in action. Action—by which is meant political action—is endowed with a mysterious capacity to generate truth. 'The primacy of action', if taken seriously, represents nothing less than an epistemological revolution. It marks the final break with Western thinking, which continues doggedly to insist on other criteria of truth and to require evidence for what is asserted. The reluctance of Western theologians to embrace with eagerness the theology of liberation is attributed to their bourgeois affluence.

The 'primacy of action' really means that political commitment is the path to truth, and the only path to truth. Since this is an unusual and disconcerting thesis, one had better trace the stages by which it came to seem plausible. The first step was to assert, with Gutiérrez, the truism that 'theology should not be cut off from life'. But note already the characteristic way in which he phrases it, and the explicit appeal to Marxism: 'We must put an end to certain types of theologians whom we can call "idealist", that is, the theologians who have nothing to do with concrete commitment. No matter how much good will he has and how much St. Augustine he has read, this type of theologian will always be an "idealist". . . . I am using the word "idealist" in the Marxist sense because only theologians who are pastorally committed match the definition of true theology' (quoted in *Marx and Jesus*, James F. Conway, Carlton Press, p. 140). Already here, theology is quite explicitly a second-order activity: 'The first thing is the commitment of charity, of service. Theology comes after' (*ibid.*, p. 141). Does this mean that theology has the task of finding reasons for what one has already decided to do on other grounds? Is it a matter of *post-factum* rationalizations? These questions are rarely raised. The next step is usually to contrast the 'Greek' view of truth, as abstract, conceptual, essentialist, with the 'Hebrew' view of truth which is 'truth-in-action'. God's word—*dabar*—does not remain inoperative, but realizes itself in action. 'Action' is thus elevated to supreme status. It provides the norm of judgment.

There can be no mistaking that this is what the theologians of liberation are really saying. 'Action' and the 'situation' are the only permitted starting points. 'The theology of liberation', declares Assmann, 'sees itself as a critical reflection on present historical practice in all its intensity and complexity', and he adds: 'Its "text" is our situation, and our situation is our primary and basic reference point' (*Practical Theology of Liberation*, p. 104). Other possible sources, such as the Bible, the teaching authority of the Church, or the history of doctrine, are secondary and do not constitute a main source of 'truth in itself'. He finds himself greatly drawn to the remark of a 'committed Christian': 'The Bible? It doesn't exist. The only bible is the sociological bible of what I see happening here and now as a Christian' (*ibid.*, p. 61). Juan Segundo speaks in similar vein: 'The only truth is the truth that is efficacious for man's liberation' (*A Theology for Artisans of a New Humanity*, Orbis, vol. IV, p. 54), and he notes that 'any orthodoxy that does not essentially point to orthopraxy is magical' (*ibid.*, vol. IV, p. 64). José Míguez Bonino accurately sums up the position of the theologians of liberation: 'They are saying, in fact, that there is no truth outside or beyond the concrete historical events in which men are involved as agents', and 'there is, therefore, no knowledge except in action itself, in the process of transforming the world through participation in history' (U.S. title *Doing Theology in a Revolutionary Age*, Fortress Press, 1975; UK title *Revolutionary Theology Comes of Age*, SPCK, 1975, p. 88). Assmann draws the conclusion, and it is inevitable in view of the preceding remarks: 'Any logic that is not practical logic is done away with' (*op. cit.*, p. 74).

It is difficult to know what to make of such statements. The 'action' that is thus privileged and exalted is obviously *political* action, but equally obviously they do not have in mind *any* kind of political action. Through the trickle of tautologies one concludes that only political actions leading to human liberation are envisaged: reactionary political actions—such as those of Nazis or Fascists—do not communicate knowledge in the same way. Now the thesis that there is no knowledge except through (the right sort of) political action brings one close to a dangerous form of irrationalism. It has already led, for example, to the rejection of 'bourgeois sociology'. Assmann maintains that 'there is no such thing as uninvolved social science, and to pretend that there is to adopt a reactionary ideological position' (*op. cit.*, p. 129). Discussion about whether sociology can be 'value-free' has been going on for a long time in the West. But Assmann uses the fact that sociology is not neutral to advocate a 'committed sociology' in which no holds are barred. He has simply exchanged one ideology for another. One thus inclines to the awful suspicion—and Bonino reminds us that Marx and Freud were the masters of suspicion—that the talk about 'the primacy of action' really indicates the primacy of the ideology in terms of which actions are judged to be tending towards or away from human liberation.

To give the theologians of liberation uncritical approval would be a way of not taking them seriously; to bother to disagree is to show the respect in which they are held. Their thesis on 'the primacy of action' depends upon a presupposition which must be explained. They assert the unity of history. There are not two parallel histories, one 'sacred' and the other 'profane', which work themselves out independently. Catholic social teaching had traditionally operated with a distinction of 'spheres' in which spiritual and temporal, though related, were not identified. Protestants since Luther had talked of two 'realms'. Such distinctions vanish in the theologians of liberation. Gutiérrez points out that there is 'only one vocation to salvation', and that it embraces all men. Consequently 'the action of man in history, whether Christian or non-Christian, gains . . . religious significance (*Theology of Liberation*, p. 72). The practical result of this way of looking at things is that political activity (provided once more it fulfils the 'right' conditions) is lent additional sanction from on high. Though it is obviously desirable that 'spirituality' should be brought down to earth and embodied, the immediate identification of God's will with a particular political position is dangerous. One can assert 'the unity of history' and of man's vocation, without always being able to say that 'the finger of God is here' in this political commitment.

The distinction between sacred and secular at least enabled Christians to remain critical of all ideologies. Conversely, where distinctions between the two realms have been allegedly abolished, the secular tends to acquire the prestige of the sacred. This can be seen in the way the Latin American theologians identify their struggle for liberation with that of the Jewish people described in the Book of Exodus. Exodus rather than the Risen Christ provides the primary model of liberation in Latin America. James F. Conway explains this in terms of the Latin

American situation: 'Christ is not yet risen for the majority of the Latin American people who still suffer misery, starvation and deprivation' (*ibid.*, p. 99). The Promised Land has not been reached. The desert has not yet been crossed. They have only just embarked on the path of liberation.

In Jewish history it was indeed impossible to distinguish between sacred and secular, between the history of salvation and the political history of the people of Israel. God's guidance and providence were expressed through events. It is not difficult to see why the theologians of liberation should be so fascinated by this phase of redemptive history. Exodus provides the scenario and Moses, an 'authentic politician', becomes the hero. On this point, Segundo Galilea notes, 'the consensus is remarkable' (*Concilium*, June 1974, p. 31, fn. 8). Here is Galilea's portrait of Moses:

If the Christian politician in Latin America is to have a spirituality adequate to his mission and commitments, he has an inspiring model in Moses. In his political activity this prophet (and the Christian politician at the present moment in the continent ought to be a prophet) kept the wider significance of his mission alive. He knew that political liberation from Egypt fitted into a much wider and more integral plan for the eschatological salvation of the people. He knew that his activity would remain always incomplete, at times frustrated, at times rejected, because the unique and definitive liberator of the people was not himself but God whose Kingdom would have no end. So he dedicated himself up to the end, because the hope that animated him came not from himself, but was renewed daily in him, in his encounter with the Lord. And is not hope the great inspiring virtue of the politician? (*Concilium*, June 1974, p. 31).

The great merit of Moses is that he provides a better model for the politically committed than Jesus does. After the passage just quoted, Galilea goes on rather apologetically: 'In a different dimension, the message delivered to us by the Messianism of

Jesus is also profoundly illuminating. In him contemplation reverts to a commitment not directly temporal, but prophetic and pastoral, with socio-political consequences, more fitted for the ministry of evangelization than for temporal political action' (*ibid.*). Whenever Christians have sought to justify political commitment, they have tended to revert to the Old Testament.

The appeal to the 'unity of history', orchestrated through the Exodus story and the example of Moses, means a fresh look at every single theological issue. Along with the distinction of sacred and secular will go other hallowed distinctions which divided the love of God from the love of one's neighbor, the Church from humanity, 'spiritual salvation' from political liberation, and the unity-bringing sacraments from general human solidarity. All dualism, says Assmann succinctly, is *reactionary*. On what used to be called the question of Church membership, Juan Segundo makes it clear that the true Body of Christ includes all those who are committed in the struggle for liberation, for faith depends not upon the 'religious situation' (i.e., whether someone happens to call himself a Christian or not) but upon his 'service to man' (*A Theology for Artisans of a New Humanity,* vol. II, p. 112). But what, then, is faith? Hugo Assmann explains: 'Faith is no more and no less than man's historical activity (which is essentially political)' (*Practical Theology of Liberation*, p. 35). In this generously accommodating view, faith is stretched to the very limit of meaningfulness. The consequence of such affirmations is that the universality of the Gospel comes to mean not so much a proclamation to be shared, but rather a declaration that the grace of the Gospel is already at work, leavening the lump of revolution and efforts towards humanization (Segundo, *ibid.*, vol. V, p. 96). Or as Gutiérrez puts it: 'The Lord is the Sower who arises at dawn to sow the field of historical reality before we establish our distinctions' (*Theology of Liberation*, p. 255). Among the discarded distinctions is that between those who wear the Christian label and those who do not, for as Gutiérrez has already stated: 'The *unqualified* affirmation of the universal salvific will has radically changed the way of conceiving the mission of the Church in the world' (*ibid.*; my italics). Gutiérrez's assumption is that

'God is at work in human history', and no Christian could quarrel with it: the problem comes when we try to specify the way this happens.

None of this adds up to Marxism in any precise form. Nevertheless Marxism is implicit all along in the assertion of the primacy of action or *praxis*, in the idea that a choice of the oppressed will lead to further knowledge, and, as we shall see, in the acceptance of class-conflict as a positive force. But Marxism is not discussed with much clarity by the theologians of liberation. They are Marxists because of the lack of any alternative analysis of society and the causes of its oppression. Their use of Marxism is instrumental, that is to say, practical rather than ideological. They would agree with Paul Lehmann when he writes that 'contemporary revolutionary practice has been forged by the Marxist assessment of the concrete mode of injustice and the realities of power', but agree further when he adds that Marxism has been 'increasingly freed of ideological bondage' (*The Transfiguration of Politics*, U.S., Harper and Row, 1974; UK, SCM Press, 1975, p. 103). In conversation with James F. Conway, Gutiérrez gave his assessment of Marxism. The hopeful dialogue discussed in the last chapter was based, he believed, on the *young* Marx, and it led to no useful conclusion other than that Christianity represented a theistic form of humanism while Marxism was an atheistic form of humanism. Thus 'the two become tragic lovers whose only solution is suicide'—unless they postpone dialogue altogether and concentrate on praxis (*Marx and Jesus*, p. 136).

Gutiérrez believes that the work of Louis Althusser, a leading French Marxist theoretician, has opened up new possibilities. For Althusser Marxism is essentially a 'science', while Marx's early thoughts on alienation and humanism represent a romantic, pre-scientific approach that he later abandoned without regret. While Althusser's views, popularized in Latin America by Marta Harnecker, put an end to the kind of dialogue practised in Europe, they made possible another form of dialogue which stressed the scientific (as opposed to ideological) character of Marxism; from this point of view, religion has no more difficulty with Marxism than it has with, say, biology.

Nevertheless, Gutiérrez hastens to explain, there remain grounds for dialogue since there is even in the later Marx an *ethical concern* which leads him in *Das Kapital* to reject the injustices of society in the name of a certain idea of *man* (*Marx and Jesus*, pp. 136-137).

The distinction between scientific analysis and ideology has enabled many Christians to look more favorably on Marxism. It seems to provide all the advantages of Marxist perceptiveness without the burden of its metaphysics. It has become very widespread, and was expressed in popular form by Dom Helder Camara: 'I think we can avail ourselves of the Marxist method of analysis which is still valid, while leaving aside the materialistic conception of life'. José Míguez Bonino has used the distinction to break down the incompatibility between Christianity and Marxism: in politics 'we move totally in the area of human rationality—in the realm where God has invited man to be *on his own*' (*Doing Theology in a Revolutionary Age*, p. 98). And if we are really moving 'in the area of human rationality', Bonino is surely right to conclude that 'the only legitimate question is whether the analysis and projection do in fact correspond to the facts of human history. If they do, and to the extent that they do, they become the *unavoidable historical mediation* of Christian obedience' (*ibid.*). That simply means that Christians have to follow the facts, wherever they lead. If Althusser's distinction between ideology and science can be sustained, then clearly a giant step will have been taken in Christian-Marxist relations, and the most fundamental obstacle to agreement will have been removed.

Thus the popularization of Althusser's view of Marxism as a science has helped some Christians to embrace Marxism, but at the same time it does not seem to give a complete account of Marxism. Gutiérrez admits this, and recognizes that operationally Marxism behaves more like a faith than a science. It impels men to action in solidarity and sustains their hope. It can mean risking one's life for one's fellow men. Can science do all this? Bonino, too, has to concede that Marxism does not always present itself in the calmly rational way he has described. 'It is frequently possessed by an apostolic zeal', he observes, 'a dogmatic certainty and a messianic fervour, the causes of which we cannot discuss here. . . . (*ibid.*, p. 98). Since so much depends on the validity of the distinction between science and ideology, that seems a faint-hearted procedure. Gutiérrez is a little more forthcoming. He attempts to solve the problem by positing, somewhere between scientific analysis and Christian faith, an intermediate level which, following Marcuse, he calls *utopia*. Althusser is chided for relegating utopia to the realm of ideology. Utopia, on the contrary, is seen positively as the vision of final liberation which both stimulates science by putting before it the project of a renewed humanity and encourages faith by stretching its imagination. Utopia is the middle term. 'Faith and political action', he explains, 'do not relate to each other except through the project of creation of a new type of man in a different society, through utopia. . . .' (*Theology of Liberation*, p. 236).

It is difficult to put any precise content into this rather misty vision, but one thing should be clear: Gutiérrez rejects one way of stating the relationship between Christianity and Marxism. He refers to a group of 'committed Christians' in Chile who delight in finding converging patterns in Christianity and Marxism. Thus Christ becomes the 'First Socialist', revolution becomes a form of redemption, auto-criticism is seen as analogous to confession, and the vision of a society in which there is 'neither Jew nor Greek' becomes a sketch for the classless society. Gutiérrez dismisses this hasty synthesizing as the attempt to make revolutionary Marxism a little more palatable by adding to it a dash of transcendental sauce (James P. Conway, *Marx and Jesus*, p. 137). But that did not put an end to the attempt, as we shall see in the next chapter.

One can put some flesh on this skeleton of theory by examining how the theologians of liberation deal with the class-war. This provides a useful test of the seriousness of their Marxism, and perhaps an indication of how far it is modified by their Christianity. Gutiérrez's starting point is that the existence of class struggle is an incontrovertible fact—all that remains is to study it: 'Its evolution, its exact extent, its nuances, and its variations are the object of analysis of the social sciences and pertain to the field of scientific rationality' (*A Theology of Libera-tion*, p. 273). The class-war does not depend upon religious or ethical options, and it cannot be spirited away by dialectical finesse. It is simply there. Gutiérrez explains that Marx did not invent the class-struggle, but rather analyzed its causes, and showed how it could be made to lead to the classless society (*ibid.*, p. 284, fn. 51). But having noted the omnipresence of the class-struggle, the next 'fact' adduced by Gutiérrez is that neutrality is impossible. Those who claim to be above the heat and smoke of the battle are deceiving themselves. They become apologists for the *status quo*. Hence the dream of the harmonious reconciliation of complementary social classes, expressed in papal social encyclicals by the term *interclassismo,* is a piece of self-deception: 'It is a classist option, deceitfully camouflaged by a purported equality before the law' (*ibid.*, p. 275). The task of the theologian of liberation, therefore, will be to unmask the complicities with power, and to rouse the working class to an awareness of the class-struggle and participation in it. No neutrality. He who is not with me is against me—and it is worth recalling that this was always Lenin's favorite Scripture quotation. Those who dissent are dupes.

To urge the class-war poses obvious problems for the Christian, who is commanded to 'love his enemies'. Gutiérrez embarks on the casuistry of the class-war, and justifies it on three grounds. To speak of 'love' in general is an abstraction. It is only realized in the concrete. It does not involve preserving a merely bogus appearance of harmony. Gutiérrez quotes Girardi with approval: 'Love for those who live in a condition of objective sin demands that we struggle to liberate them from it. The liberation of the poor and the liberation of the rich are achieved simultaneously' (*Violenze dei Cristiani*, p. 122). Secondly, the challenge of the Gospel is how to combine 'real and effective combat', but without hatred: 'It is not a question of having no enemies, but rather of not excluding them from our love'. But love does not mean that they are no longer enemies. Thirdly, love is not authentic if it does not take the form of class solidarity and social struggle. This principle is opposed to that of universal love only if we take a short-term view, for class-struggle

is seen as the only way to make universal love effective today:
'For this participation is what leads to a classless society without owners and dispossessed, without oppressors and oppressed.
In dialectical thinking, reconciliation is the overcoming of conflict' (*ibid.*, p. 276). Conflict and its expression in violence are
provisional, a means to a loving goal. Gutiérrez concludes that
the task of the Church is to 'politicize by evangelizing' (p. 269).
And he recognizes that in the Latin American context this
means subversion (p. 270).

The apology for the class-war colours all subsequent judgments. It extends to an analysis of the fictitious 'unity' of the
Church as it exists today. Segundo maintains that the idea of
sacramental communion is an illusion which leads the Church
'to lose any and all specific import and significance' (*A Theology for Artisans of a New Humanity*, IV, p. 10). He believes that
it is impossible to remain in communion with those 'who think
and do things that are completely different', or those who are
manifestly in opposition to what God is doing in the world
(*ibid.*, III, pp. 78-79). Let them be anathema. The conclusion is
that the Church should place all its declining resources on the
side of revolutionary change, and should not be hindered by dis-
tracting notions about Christian unity (*ibid.*, IV, pp. 132 *et
seq.*).

The theology of liberation leads, then, to a clear political
conclusion, and its main function is to provide a rationale for
that conclusion. It declares that the 'option for socialism' has
become a Christian moral imperative for Latin America, indeed
the moral imperative. 'Socialism' is often used as a vague ges-
ture towards hope. Dom Helder Camara says: 'My socialism is
a special one which respects the human person and turns to the
Gospel. My socialism is justice' (quoted in *Doing Theology in a
Revolutionary Age*, p. 47). Few could be so perverse as to disagree with that. Juan Segundo defines 'socialism' rather more
precisely as 'a political regime in which the ownership of the
means of production is removed from individuals and handed
over to higher institutions whose concern is the common good'
(*Concilium*, June 1974, p. 115). But there is no hint as to
whether this desirable result is to be achieved through 'democratic centralism' (a euphemism for Party control) or self-

government on the local level (the Yugoslav model). However, Segundo knows enough utterly to reject 'capitalism' by which he means 'a regime in which the ownership of the goods of production is open to economic competition.' He does not consider the possibility that there might be countries which have a 'mixed economy', but he insists that the choice is not between society as it exists in the U.S.A. or in the Soviet Union. Latin America will have to find its own original solutions, trace its own path to liberation. No existing models will be of any help.

The theology of liberation with its high hopes, its sincerity, its slogans, its biblical parallels and Marxist borrowings is a Latin American phenomenon in its origins and development. But it has been extended patchily to other regions of the 'third world' where oppressive regimes are encountered, notably in the Pacific islands. A formal attempt was made to introduce it to the United States in August-September 1975 when a six-day conference was held in Detroit. There was much anguished breast-beating from those who discovered that they had been oppressors all along. Its relevance to the American 'suburban Mass-goer' was doubted, but Fr. Donald Hessler reported that there were a number of 'profound conversions'. He quoted one suburbanite: 'Now I see. We are not to go to the poor to teach them, nor to learn from them, but we go to the poor and oppressed to share their insecurity, to struggle at their side and to pray with them.' But he admitted that the slogan 'No Liberation without Adoration' did not match the general mood. Gutiérrez appeared in person to explain that violence was advocated only reluctantly as the answer to 'institutionalized violence' which 'assassinates and kills more children than any other form of violence in Latin America.' The only permissible violence was counter-violence. But this did not prevent an editorial in the *National Catholic Reporter* from remarking that 'instead of Isaiah's exhortation to turn swords into ploughshares, liberation theology turns altar rails into barricades' (5 September 1975). Blacks, Asians, Hispano-Americans, Appalachians, and women all pressed their claim to be considered oppressed groups, so that as the detailed forms of oppression proliferated, the content of liberation became more elusive.

This development had been foreshadowed by Rosemary

Radford Ruether who had extended the analysis of pernicious dualism to cover the whole range of human life. Dualism has characterized the 'Western design of consciousness' and split reality into false polarities: it has privileged masculinity over femininity, man (ruling-class male) over creation, spirit over body, self over society, heaven over earth. These dualities are false not only because they keep apart what should be united, but because 'God' is used to reinforce the upper pole of each contrast. Liberation theology, in each of its modes, consists in the unmasking of this process. It becomes, therefore, an assault on the 'reality principle' of Western consciousness ('Whatever Happened to Theology?' in *Christianity and Crisis*, 12 May 1975). Ms. Ruether's analysis shows the possible range of liberation theology. But she is less concerned with the polarity which matters most for the third world: the contrast between the oppressors and the oppressed in the social and political sphere. It is this contrast that is emphasized by 'Christians for Socialism'.

4
Christians For Socialism

The theology of liberation would have been false to itself if it had merely gestured and exhorted in the direction of action. It could not remain an inert theory, without any impact on life. It was embodied in practical political form in the movement called Christians For Socialism (henceforward CFS) which may be said to have come into official existence at a conference held in Santiago, Chile, from 23 to 30 April 1972. It was in principle an international conference and reports were presented from Argentina, Bolivia, Peru, Uruguay (the Tupamaros) and Chile itself. The Brazilians had been refused passports, and a delegation from Quebec reported on '200 years of dependence, oppression and humiliation'. Msgr. Sergio Mendez Arceo, Bishop of Cuernavaca in Mexico, was the only episcopal representative, though nearly two-thirds of the four hundred delegates were priests. By a nice irony of timing the Conference coincided with a meeting of UNCTAD which was also held in Santiago. It was therefore set against the developed world's manifest incapacity to adjust the terms of world trade in favor of the developing world. In an opening address Fr. Gonzalo Arroyo, S.J., said that the purpose of the Conference was to reflect theologically on the revolutionary commitment of Christians, 'which in many cases runs the risk of being mere activism'. A message from President Salvador Allende welcomed the delegates and made clear the immense symbolic importance of the Conference for Chile. 'Divisions today', declared the Chilean President, 'are not on the religious level or on the level of philosophic ideas; the real division is between imperialism and dependent countries'.

Thus, though the Conference was by no means exclusively

Chilean, it reflected the situation in Chile where, for the first time in history, a predominantly Communist government had come to power by legitimate and democratic means. Salvador Allende's left-wing coalition, *Unidad Popular*, had narrowly won the presidential election of September 1970, securing 36.9% of the votes as against 34.9% of the extreme right. Chile, along with Cuba, became a symbol for Latin America. Hence the importance of President Fidel Castro's visit in November and December 1971. Castro traversed the 'absurd geography' of Chile from end to end, kissing babies, clowning at basketball, and declared that 'Chile is like a good movie—you never want to leave'. He also conferred several times with Cardinal Silva Henriquez of Santiago, who thoughtfully presented him with a Bible. Castro's most important statement for Christian-Marxist relations was that the revolutionary character of Christianity should be recognized. It had begun as the religion of the poor and the oppressed, and it could revert to that role. The Cuban revolution, he claimed, had never been anti-Catholic nor anti-Christian nor anti-religious. A priest, Fr. Sardina, had been among his troops. It was Castro's first visit to a Latin American country in eleven years.

Castro's assertions on the possibility of co-operation found a richly prepared soil. Cardinal Silva Henriquez had demonstrated that he was not on principle hostile to the regime: he was ostentatiously present at the *Te Deum* on the day of Allende's inauguration; he attended a workers' rally on 1 May 1971 in Plaza Bulnes; with the other Bishops he had supported the take-over of the copper industry. Despite this, the Chilean Bishops had not 'sold out' to Marxism. In a position paper called *The Gospel, Politics and Socialism*, fruit of their joint reflections at Temuco in April 1971, they showed their respect for the regime legitimately established in Chile, but at the same time made clear their opposition to doctrinaire Marxism. Capitalism, they agreed, was selfish and had gravely damaged Chilean society, but they warned against the philosophical errors of Marxism, particularly its materialism. 'Marxism', they said, 'ignores and denies those dimensions of man that are important for the Christian: his spiritual transcendence and his openness

to God'. Its analysis of society 'appears to lead directly to a
type of practical atheism'. Finally, it sees man in limited economic terms, and thus Marxism in effect makes the same mistake as capitalism: it values a man for 'what he does' rather
than for 'what he is'. With this critique of the philosophical
roots of Marxism, however, went the assertion that Christians
could collaborate with Marxists in building a more human society, provided a new form of Marxism, pluralist, less dogmatic
and more humanistic, was developed.

Meanwhile, in the hurly-burly of everyday politics, the
ideological conflict was becoming sharper and more virulent.
Unidad Popular was finding its program difficult to realize. In
April 1971 it secured 50% of the vote in communal elections—
of minimal practical importance but of great symbolic value.
This evidence of popular support led the Christian Democrats,
who had hitherto hoped to play the role of referee between the
extreme right and the popular front, to swing to the right. CFS
arose out of this historical context. It had three main functions.
First it would provide Christian support for the Allende government. Secondly, it would undercut the objection that Christianity and Marxism were incompatible by demonstrating that
there actually were Christians who were also Marxists. They did
not see Christianity as the private possession of late capitalism,
still less as the ideology of the Christian Democratic Party
(whether of the centre or the right). The episcopal critique of
Marxism was dismissed as based on out-moded views and mass-
media dominated stereotypes which continued to link Marxism
with totalitarianism in a way that was contrary to the experience of the Chilean people. These views had already been expressed by the *Ochenta* group and in particular by Gonzalo Arroyo.

The third function of CFS was to forestall a right-wing
exploitation of Christianity by showing that there was in practice an unconscious alliance between Christianity and bourgeois
ideology. This had to be unmasked. So CFS counter-attacked.
Faced with the argument that Christianity and Marxism were
incompatible, they replied that Christianity and capitalism were
most certainly incompatible. All these themes were orchestrated

in the Manifesto of CFS produced by the Santiago Conference. It was not a meeting of fun-revolutionaries engaged on a joy-ride. Some of those present had been in prison. Yet there was a mood of optimism, and bliss it was that dawn to be alive. 'The air was dense', reported one of the participants, 'with the dyna-mism and buoyancy of a common purpose' (José Miguez Bonino, *Doing Theology in a Revolutionary Situation*, Fortress Press, 1975/*Revolutionary Theology Comes of Age*, SPCK, 1975, p. xx). 'We did not expect to depart', Bonino added, 'car-rying a mere set of well-meaning resolutions, but an adequate instrument for the struggle' (*ibid.*). They departed in fact with a Manifesto which made explicit use of Marxism as an *analysis*:

> The construction of socialism cannot be achieved by means of vague denunciations or appeals to good will; it presup-poses an analysis that will highlight the mechanisms which really drive society. Political action calls for a scientific analysis of reality, for there is a continuous inter-relation between action and analysis (11).

History can only be understood, CFS explains, in terms of class-conflict: revolutionary praxis has revealed that any objec-tive and scientific interpretation of history must have recourse to class analysis as its key. This special insight into history has 'its own specific rationality, qualitatively different from the ra-tionality of bourgeois social sciences' (32). Marxism has help-fully provided the tools for 'conscientization', for the awakening of the masses (32). Beyond a merely short-term tactical alliance between Christians and Marxists, there is need of a long-term strategic alliance. However, there are twitches of independent thinking: building socialism is not just a matter of applying a 'dogmatic blue-print' to situations, and socialism is not simply a collection of historical doctrines but rather 'a critical theory which is always in development' (52). 'The Cuban revolution', adds the Manifesto, 'and the Chilean march towards socialism raise the question of the need for a return to Marxist sources and a critique of traditional dogmatic Marxism' (31).

Clearly a consciously Marxist document, the Manifesto

was also explicitly presented as a Christian contribution to the revolution. The question was no longer the abstract one about compatibility: CFS declared positively that they drew upon the resources of their Christian faith and found there a motivation to work for the transformation of society. This is the form the 'imitation of Christ' takes today:

> It is not enough to base a diagnosis on the facts of injustice. Christ, for example, taught us to *live* what he proclaimed. He preached human brotherhood and a love which should penetrate all the structures of society, but above all he lived out his message of liberation to the uttermost. He was condemned to death. The men of power of his time understood that his message of liberation and the effective love he showed would seriously threaten their economic, social, political and religious interests. The Spirit of the Risen Christ is today more active than ever: he provides the dynamism of history, and finds expression in all those who give themselves in solidarity in the struggle for liberty and show an authentic love of their oppressed brothers (5).

The Manifesto asserts the profound unity of human history. Distinctions between 'religious' and 'secular' vanish as Christ is seen at work in 'liberating events', though it is conceded that his presence is not limited to such events (9). The tragedy is that those Christians who are prisoners of bourgeois ideology impede the action of Christ in the world. They turn Christianity into an instrument of 'cultural oppression' in so far as they develop a spirituality which is individualistic, escapist, and misled by the false ideal of the preservation of unity at all costs. The dream of a Church without conflict helps to preserve the *status quo*. CFS, on the other hand, do not fear conflict and want to force it out into the open. They are convinced that 'the revolutionary struggle unmasks the fictitious unity of the Church today and so prepares the true unity of the Church tomorrow' (68).

The trouble was that 'unmasking the fictitious unity of the

Church today' looked to some observers suspiciously like rending it apart, while 'the true unity of the Church tomorrow' remained a distant pipe-dream, inaccessible until everyone had been converted to the views of CFS. At a press conference in Santiago, Bishop Mendez Arceo attempted to answer some of the commonest objections to their positions. He repeated the by now routine distinction between Marxism as 'scientific analysis', which he accepted, and Marxism as a philosophical system, which he rejected. Atheism belonged to the philosophical luggage of Marxism, and was not essential to it. 'God', he explained, 'has not revealed any social science'. In the poor and the oppressed there is 'a theophany of the Lord', and to stand with them in solidarity 'is the clearest sign that the Messianic Kingdom has come'. He denounced the way Christian Democratic Parties had tended to exploit Christianity while absolutizing a certain form of democracy. Bishop Mendez Arceo justified revolutionary violence as a legitimate response to 'the institutionalized violence of repressive societies', though he was careful to add that violence was not the only way to change. Asked about 'the likelihood of success' as a criterion for the use of violence (a parallel to the criterion of 'success' in traditional 'just war' theory), he quoted the example of Camilo Torres. Torres did not seriously imagine that the guerrilla movement he joined was on the verge of taking power in Bogotà: 'The success that he sought was simply to bear witness'. The Gospel, concluded the Bishop, is 'explosive, very explosive, because it relativizes everything'.

Although CFS grew out of the precise needs of the Chilean situation, its analysis was resolutely universal in scope and was extended to cover the whole world. The word 'global' occurs with striking frequency in the Manifesto. The project for the transformation of society is 'global' (47). The mechanism of oppression in Latin America is 'global' (8). 'Global' and rational planning of the economy, which presupposes the expropriation of all the means of production and finance, is urgently required (52). Christian faith, by stimulating the revolutionary ferment, confirms the project of the 'global' transformation of society (65). Bishop Mendez Arceo said that the Gospel 'relativizes everything', but it does not appear to make any impact on the underlying Marxist analysis of society which is immune to criticism. It remained to extend the analysis to the whole world. This step was taken by Fr. Gonzalo Arroyo, after he had been exiled from Chile. He possesses a single explanatory key of universal applicability. So anxious is he to divide the world into oppressors and oppressed that he rejects the term 'third world' as misleading, disruptive of the dialectic, and describes the stark alternative in these terms:

> On the one hand there is an *international bourgeoisie* of which the national bourgeoisies of the poor capitalist countries form just as much a part as those of the rich capitalist ones. . . . On the other hand there is an international proletariat, of which the industrial and agricultural workers of the rich capitalist countries are just as much a part as those of the poor capitalist countries. . . . In this context of a world divided into two and not three, the only rational solution to the structural crisis of the international capitalist system comes from socialism. . . . To survive, humanity must choose between destruction and socialism ('Christians for Socialism', interview in *New Blackfriars*, November 1974, p. 491).

Arroyo is evidently aware of opposition to these ideas within the Church. He is neither surprised nor particularly pained by it: he regards it as the obvious result of the fact that the churches are 'the institutional allies of capitalism' and therefore prisoners. But he does not wish to break with the Church. His hope is that CFS will win an increasing number of adherents in the Church who will come to see political commitment 'as a service to the authentic message of Jesus Christ which summons Christians to identify themselves with the oppressed, struggling for their liberation and simultaneously for the liberation of all mankind' (*ibid.*, p. 498). That is the prophetic task within the Church. Arroyo does not speak of 'Marxism', and in the circumstances he hardly needs to. However, he is not a 'reductionist' and asserts that the main task is to show 'by our practice, as much as by our words, that the Christian faith can and must become more and more at home in a socialist option, *even if it cannot become enclosed within that option*' (my italics).

The military coup of September 1973 put an end to CFS in Chile. Most of its leaders went underground or were imprisoned or exiled. But by then CFS had become a loosely structured international movement which developed particularly in countries where the Church had exercised a strong social role in the past and felt the need of repentance for past mistakes. Marxism, remarked Bernard Levin, owes much of its success to 'a superior capacity to induce guilt'. The movement launched in Latin America flowed back to Europe, where it linked up with existing groups such as the Italian 'basic communities', the Spanish underground movement, *Frères du Monde* in France and *Slant* in Britain. Left-wing Christian groups which had been floundering or petering out after the disappointment of 1968, when the revolution failed to come, were given a new lease of life and a new hope. In particular the Spanish and Italian CFS both held conferences in which one can see the application of the ideas expressed at Santiago to their own situations. There is much borrowing, and the movement seems to operate within a very narrow circle of ideas. This helps the task of exposition.

The Spaniards met in January 1973. In order to put the police off the scent, a misleading date and venue were published, and though the meeting is known as the 'Congress of Avila', in fact it met somewhere near Barcelona. The 200 Spanish CFS declare that they are not mere 'fellow-travellers' but intend to be fully committed to 'the realisation of the objective task of the proletariat: the constitution of a socialist society and the decisive struggle against capitalist exploitation' (text in *Dialog*, 3, 1974, pp. 235 *et seq.*). Though they waste little time on the niceties of theological debate, the Spaniards take the trouble to explain that in their opinion 'the resurrection of Jesus Christ only takes on its full meaning when every form of exploitation of man by man has ceased'. They have been taught by Marxism that this is 'the only way to make the liberating message of the Gospel effective'. They concede that in the past a Christian who became a militant Marxist had to give up his

faith, but find that to be no longer true today: 'We start from
the assumption that the contradiction between faith and Marxist commitment has not yet been overcome, but it *can be overcome* in the struggle for liberation'. *Solvitur ambulando.* They
have already learned 'with great and liberating clarity that
Christ himself lived and died a victim of the powerful oppressors of his time'; that 'the sharing in the class struggle makes
possible a genuine and effective love of one's neighbor'; and
that the class struggle is waged within the Church itself, a process that must be 'unmasked' (i.e., its true nature must be revealed). The lessons to be learned from Marxism are not
matched by any corresponding contribution of Christianity.

The Spaniards were working in haste and clandestinity.
The Italian CFS had more leisure and ten times as many people
to work on their Bologna Manifesto in September 1973. They
produced a lengthy document which shows some awareness of
complexities. They start from the imperative need for a class
choice (*una scelta di classe*). This term was consciously intended
to be the rejection of *interclassismo*, the expression used in
papal social encyclicals to evoke the idea of harmonious co-
operation between social classes. They then denounce the bank-
ruptcy of 'Christian social teaching' and the alliance of the
Church with Christian Democracy and therefore with capitalism. Having made their class choice, they discover that they are
not the first in the field. The working class has given itself an instrument: the Marxist analysis and revolutionary praxis, which
constitute the knowledge of the proletariat—a knowledge that
knows and discovers the world even as it transforms it' (text in
Dialog, 3, 1974, pp. 237-244). But if this privileged knowledge is
not to remain inert and theoretical, it must make use of 'the or-
ganizations of the working classes'. The Italian CFS chastely
avoid mentioning the Communist Party by name, no doubt
because of the divergencies on the left in Italy. They loyally
recognize the existence of such divisions, assert optimistically
that 'they must be solved' (without saying how), but insist that
they do not want to replace one kind of Catholic authoritarianism by another. Having rejected the attempt to exploit the
Gospel to legitimate the established order, they do not propose

to exploit it again as the legitimation of revolution. The Gospel is politically neutral. No unambiguous 'social doctrine' can be deduced from it.

However, having made this distinction, the Italian CFS immediately add that 'there can be no neutral reading of the Gospel, since the way one reads it depends on one's class position'. 'We discover', they explain, 'how to read the Bible in a new way —from the point of view of the oppressed and the poor', and this new reading uncovers the original meaning of the Gospel and its 'repressed truths'. They admit that the rediscovery of the subversive potential of the Gospel poses a dilemma: either Christianity must be given up, or it must be lived in a new way. They—solemnly—declare their conviction that 'beyond the contradictions, whose importance we do not underestimate, there is fundamental agreement between the imperatives which come to us from faith and those which come from our revolutionary commitment'. The two imperatives are united 'in a dialectical relationship of mutual criticism and mutual fruitfulness'.

The Italian CFS have been at the centre of a storm of controversy. They have been attacked and they have counter-attacked. The initial onslaught came in *Civiltà Cattolica*, the semi-official review of the Italian Jesuits, in a series of articles by Fr. Bartolomeo Sorge (cf. 'Ambiguity of Christians for Socialism', 21 September 1974, and 'Three Questions for Christian Marxists', 19 July 1975). Sorge's main complaint is that the Christian Marxists have not faced up to grave problems to which their attempted synthesis inevitably leads. He mentions three in particular. The first is that the acceptance of the validity of the Marxist analysis of society leads one to consider the Church as the ally of capitalism. The Church claims to stand above the contending parties: but neutrality in the class-war is impossible; and therefore the Church is in fact aligned with capitalism. He who is not with me is against me. Hence Sorge's first question: 'How can one continue to belong to the Church if one sees in it the class enemy that must be opposed by every possible means, and with which no accommodation can be found?' To say that small, prophetic groups within the Church are already anticipating a future in solidarity with the working-classes is an insufficient answer, since the Church taken as a whole does not regard them as a good guide to the future.

Sorge's second question concerns the Marxist thesis that the 'ideological superstructure', of which religion is a part, is determined by the economic base. If religion can be 'explained' in this way, 'how is one to preserve the transcendence, the supra-historical and supernatural character of Christianity?' Finally Sorge challenges the 'materialistic' reading of the Bible which, he claims, reduces Jesus to 'a mere man'. He concedes that a study of the socio-economic conditions in the time of Jesus can throw light on his message, but rejects the idea that this approach provides a key to the understanding of the New Testament. Sorge's articles set the tone for subsequent episcopal attacks on CFS, though they have been chiefly remarkable for their vagueness. In December 1975 the Episcopal Vicar of Rome, Msgr. Poletti, who has pastoral charge of the Rome diocese on behalf of the Pope, revived the argument that 'one cannot be simultaneously Marxist and Christian'. In an interview in the Rome *Daily American* he said: 'The fact that Italy is prepared to place her hope in an atheistic doctrine is a cause of profound sorrow and concern for all beginning with the Holy Father'. The unity of the Italian episcopate was still further secured by the sacking of Salvatore Baldassari, Archbishop of Ravenna, who was widely known as 'the Red Archbishop'. After months of pressure, he resigned on grounds of 'ill-health', seven years before reaching the age limit of seventy-five.

It seemed that the clock had been put back. Pope John XXIII had not allowed his thinking to be dominated by Italian considerations. He had received in audience Khrushchev's son-in-law, Alexis Adjoubei, an indiscretion which the right-wing press claimed was to lose a million votes for the Christian Democrats. Pope John's eye was on the wider international scene. But throughout the 1960's and 1970's the Italian Communist Party was gradually gaining strength with each successive election. Under the suave leadership of Enrico Berlinguer it had asserted its independence of Moscow, tried to reassure the electorate of its democratic reliability, and held out the hand of friendship to the Christian Democrats by proposing a 'historic compromise' or alliance. As the election fixed for 20 June 1976 drew near, ecclesiastical pronouncements multiplied. Six prominent Catholics decided to stand with the Communists, and they were supported by a letter from six hundred priests, academics, and trade unionists. This indiscipline brought down thunder on their heads. The Italian Episcopal Conference met in May 1976, and its president, Cardinal Poma, issued another strong statement: 'We recall once again the theoretical and practical irreconcilability of Christianity and atheistic communism, and consequently of a man's profession of Christian faith and his association with and support for any recognized Marxist movement, *even when he insists that he does not share its ideological outlook*'. The last phrase was clearly directed at CFS. Cardinal Poma went on to hint at the possibility of excommunication: 'This is a fatherly warning and a heartfelt appeal for united witness to the one faith and full communion, in the context of which alone sharing in the one Eucharist and collaboration in the one evangelizing mission of the Church can be permitted'. In his address to the Episcopal Conference, Pope Paul backed up this position in words which were tortuous in form, but clear enough in intention: 'It seems to us even less in line with one's civic, moral, social and religious duties, and therefore less tolerable to align oneself, particularly in public, with political attitudes which, by reason of their ideological content and as historical experience has shown, are radically opposed to our religious concept of life'. Despite these exhortations, the Communist Party won 34.4% of the votes and were only just beaten by the 38.7% won by the Christian Democrats. The episcopal and papal interventions had fallen on deaf ears.

But if appeals to authority proved ineffectual, Fr. Sorge's attempt to produce arguments against CFS had no more success, except among those who did not need any convincing. There was a *dialogue des sourds* in which everyone was shouting and no one was listening. A typical reply to Fr. Sorge came from Pietro Brugnoli, formerly Professor at the Gregorian University (in 'Scelta Socialista ed esperanza di fede', IDOC, November 1974, pp. 48-54). Not only does Brugnoli reject the charges, as one might expect, but he attempts to demonstrate

the link between being a Christian and being a Marxist (what
Bologna called 'mutual fruitfulness'). He claims that we have
got our idea of God all wrong, and that we need to 'change
God' ('*cambiare Dio*'): the God of the Bible is the Lord of justice who vindicates the oppressed. The biblical way of looking
at the world is not reconciling and does not advocate harmony
between classes; on the contrary it is marked by conflict and
dialectic. God is not neutral. He is the Lord proclaimed in the
Gospels who casts down the mighty from their thrones, exalts
the humble, fills the hungry with good things, and sends the rich
away empty-handed. The countdown of the *Magnificat* has already begun.

Clearly when one has evolved this 'alternative' concept of
God, it becomes impossible to make him the prop and guaran-
tor of an unjust social system. Brugnoli concludes that CFS are
socialists not 'in spite of their Christian faith' but in accordance
with 'the logic of Christian faith'. And if one enquires about the
'specific contribution' of Christianity (a legitimate question,
unless 'mutual fruitfulness' means nothing at all), Brugnoli re-
plies that as far as *content* goes, there is none. The 'extra' factor, the *più*, the specifically Christian dimension is found in the
motivations provided by faith and hope, and in the *ultimate* significance of this struggle. For out of the struggle in favour of
humanity, a new Church is emerging, an alternative Church determined from below.

But the alternative Church has not yet emerged, and its
outline is so far unclear. One of the leading theoreticians of
CFS, Giulio Girardi, whom we last met lecturing Marxists at
Chiemsee in Chapter 2, stated the central question of Marxist-
Christian relationship in its sharpest form when he wrote:

If it is true that a Christian can be a revolutionary, one still
has to explain why a revolutionary should be a Christian.
The question is no longer whether Christianity is compatible with Marxism, but whether it is superfluous once
Marxism is accepted. One no longer asks whether Christianity is a hindrance to the revolution, but whether it can
contribute to it ('Nouveauté chrétienne et nouveauté du

monde', in *Lumière et Vie,* 1974, no. 116, p. 99).

In other words, faith can only hope to survive if it can make a positive contribution to the 'revolution'. If not, it is superfluous, and can be expected to disintegrate. Having posed the key question, Girardi does not stay to answer it with any clarity. He is convinced that the deliberate choice of a class point of view is an indispensable condition for understanding political and social action: adopt this point of view, and everything will fall into place. He is thus led to embrace 'scientific Marxism' as a 'system-changing strategy', but does not feel obliged to accept the official interpretation of Marxism provided by the Communist Parties. This is a typical, but not universal, judgment. CFS tend to be 'dissidents of the left', too 'revisionist' and unreliable to be really trusted by their political allies. The Christian Marxists are thus caught in a dilemma: if, out of genuine conviction and to reassure other Christians that they are nobody's dupes, they assert their independence from the Communist Party, they can be accused of 'factionalism' and splitting the left; but if, on the other hand, they pledge unconditional support to the Communist Party, then their independence is forfeited and their claim to make a 'positive contribution' is revealed as a hollow sham.

Girardi tried to maintain his independence as a free-lance Marxist. But an editorial in the German review *Dialog* took up a more submissive position. The editorial is a brisk attack on members of the German CFS movement who, at a Congress in Lyons in November 1973, had not only 'shown a certain reserve' towards official Marxist parties but had actually given vent to anti-Communist sentiments. They are taken to task for this effrontery, and for the following revealing reason: 'Since Christians For Socialism were not the first to commit themselves effectively to a more just and peaceful world, but on the contrary are only now joining in a movement whose members have already suffered and sacrificed not a little for these goals, one feels bound to ask these critics just how serious they are and how far they are merely playing academic games' ('Christen für den Sozialismus: Geschichte, Motive, Merkmale', in *Dialog*, 1974, 3, p. 197). And one feels bound to ask the three signatories of the editorial—Fernando Castillo, Kuno Füsel and Herbert Vorgrimler—just how serious *they* are. The premise of the argument is that the Communists have borne the heat and burden of the day in the struggle for peace and justice; and the conclusion is that CFS, as workers who arrive in the vineyard at the twenty-third hour, must meekly succumb to the Communist Party and stifle their criticism. There must be no question, the authors add, of setting up alternative political parties, since that would split still further the already fragmented left.

It is more usual to claim to be independent of the Communist Party. Where Marxism is embraced, it is accompanied by a qualifying and restrictive adjective. For the Santiago Conference, 'socialism' is 'a *critical* theory that is always developing' (52). Girardi wanted a '*scientific* Marxism' unencumbered by ideological nonsense. These aspirations correspond to what Paul Lehmann called '*instrumental* Marxism'. A common feature of modern revolutions is, he explains, 'an instrumental, as distinct from a dogmatic, appropriation of Marxism-Leninism, and, as its corollary, an instrumental in distinction from a dogmatic appropriation of ideology' (*The Transformation of Politics*, Harper and Row, 1974/SCM Press, 1975, p. 106). An 'instrumental' use of Marxism involves picking and choosing in the heritage of Marxism. It means being selective. It is self-evidently welcome, at least in the general sense that 'non-dogmatism' is to be preferred to 'dogmatism' which, in popular usage, means being inflexible and crassly ideological. On the other hand, it is extremely difficult to talk with those who hold an 'instrumental' version of Marxism, since one can never predict in advance the extent of their revisionism. One advantage of such an interpretation of Marxism is that it not only escapes conventional forms of attack, but that it escapes all forms of attack, since perpetual redefinition can shift the ground to be defended. In Italy the sense of an argument being pursued at cross-purposes has been greatly heightened since it is not only CFS who claim to be revisionist but the Communist Party itself. It has declared itself in favor of pluralism and democracy. It has shown itself to be fair and just in the administration of cities like Bologna where it has held power. It has not been afraid to distress the Russians: it complained about the invasion of Czechoslovakia and almost wrecked the European Communist summit in June 1976 by its noisy assertions of independence.

Yet not everyone is convinced, and the argument about the 'sincerity' and trustworthiness of the European Communist Parties continues unabated. Two contradictory assessments are made. For the Vatican, the leopard has not really changed its spots: the changes are cosmetic and the attractive new language is merely a matter of electoral tactics. The mask will be thrown off at a later stage. CFS, on the other hand, claim that there is a real change on a profound level within Marxism: it has become a tool of interpretation, an instrument for changing society, and it is no longer lumbered with atheism, dialectical materialism and the other metaphysical speculations which have historically accompanied it. The existence of CFS depends upon the validity of this assessment. If it is correct, the Vatican is simply talking about a different Marxism. Its strictures do not apply. They are aimed at the wrong target. They are based on a misunderstanding of the 'modern' and 'instrumental' Marxism that is emerging. Worse still, by maintaining out-dated stereotypes, they will delay or prevent its emergence. Which assessment is supported by the evidence? An attempt will be made to answer this question in Chapter 6.

Meanwhile it is clear that the synthesis made by CFS between Christianity and Marxism, proclaimed at Santiago and developed still further in Europe, presupposes a Marxism specially tailored to their needs. A certain amount of wish-fulfilment clouds their perception. Thus Fr. Laurence Bright. O.P., disposes neatly of atheism in two swift sentences: 'Marx, unfortunately, accepted Feuerbach's theory that God is a projection of human need. I doubt if anyone could be found today who would argue in its favor' (Letter in *The Tablet*, 23 August 1975, p. 799). He could easily be introduced to many who would gladly argue in its favor. 'Instrumental' Marxism is modified Marxism. But there is also, on the Christian Left, an 'instrumental' use of Christianity: just as Marxism is 'used' selectively, so the heritage of Christianity is pillaged for supporting arguments.

The revolutionary potential of the *Magnificat* is well brought out, but the fact that Jesus refused every kind of political power —and lost many disciples on that account—is ignored. Indeed, the 'instrumental' use of Christianity becomes quite explicit in the repeated exhortations to read the Gospels 'from a class point of view'. Of course it is possible, and stimulating, to read the Gospels 'from a class point of view', but the exclusive use of this method cannot be expected to yield up the complete mean-ing of the Gospels. There is here a not so subtle invitation to give way to ideological thinking: look at the world through these spectacles, and it will soon begin to take on a Marxist shape.

One does not have to be a blinkered reactionary to be worried by this question-begging mode of reasoning. The syn-thesis between Christianity and Marxism gains in plausibility only where there is an 'instrumental' understanding of both, and it depends upon a preliminary process of selection. This does not mean that it is false. But it does mean that it is precarious and liable to crack under strain. Lenin advised that one should always keep in mind the question: who-whom? Who is exploit-ing whom? Which is the determining, crucial element in the syn-thesis? Which gives way in case of conflict? Or are CFS right in believing that conflict cannot arise? No laboratory experiment can be devised to answer such questions, and by the time life has answered them, it will be too late to turn back. The road from Santiago is long and circuitous. There is a diversion by way of Peking.

5
Christians and the China Experience

Despite the greatest missionary effort ever mounted by the Christian Churches, the proportion of Christians among the Chinese never rose above one per cent. Before Mao's revolution, Catholics numbered about two million, and there were nearly a million and a half Protestants and Protestant 'sympathisers'. Chinese Christians were well provided with schools, universities, charitable institutions and hospitals. Through these 'works' the missionaries hoped to help the Chinese in their task of nation-building. With the coming of Mao Tse-tung in 1949, the whole enterprise collapsed. The Catholic Church no longer has any visible presence in China. One church, it is true, remains open in Peking. It is intended for foreign diplomats who witness an impeccably sung Tridentine Mass celebrated in Latin by elderly Chinese priests. Throughout the rest of China churches have been turned into atheistic schools, museums, workshops and lecture halls. The famous basilica on the Zosé Hill near Shanghai is an observatory. The twenty or so legitimate bishops who were alive in 1949 have disappeared without trace. The forty-two 'patriotic' bishops, consecrated with the government's approval in 1956-57, have likewise vanished. Visitors who ask questions about the state of religion in China are looked at with some incredulity by their guides, and regarded as faintly mad ('Dans la Chine de Mao', Henry Fesquet in *Le Monde*, 30 December 1975). There have been unverifiable reports about Christian groups meeting in secret to read the Bible or say the rosary. More ascertainable is the evidence of anti-Christian posters: one of them showed Lin Piao, once Mao's designated successor but now discredited, holding aloft a cross inscribed with the word 'Capitalism', while Confucius kneels below in smiling ecstasy. Any notion of the kind of dialogue described in Chapter 2 is hopeless. 'Nor is there any realistic prospect', wrote Fr. Parig Digan, 'that any Chinese Garaudy will trace a path "from anathema to dialogue", much less that any Chinese Solzhenitsyn will raise a Christian voice in China to call the regime in question from within' ('China and the Churches', *Pro Mundi Vita*, 55, 1975, p. 13). The failure of the Christian churches in China seems complete, and the future bleak.

Yet Christians have remained fascinated by China and reluctant to write off one-fifth of the world's population. The institutional Church may be invisible, but that does not mean that God is no longer at work in China, or even, as Victor Hayward, who was secretary of the China Study Project of the British Council of Churches, phrased it, 'mightily at work in China'. China gradually forced Christians to ask themselves searching questions about the nature of Christian mission and the mistakes that had been made, and to reflect more profoundly on the divine disguises. It was not merely a rationalization of disaster which prompted those Christians who cared about China to measure God's action there not by the number of converts made but by the assimilation of Christian values which, properly apprehended, are inseparable from human values. The questions changed. No longer did Christians anxiously wonder when the Church would be re-established in China or whether the doors of China would once more be open to missionaries. Instead, as Fr. Hubert Dargan noted, they began to ask: 'How can the contemporary Church, with its renewed understanding of itself, meet contemporary China? Have they any aspirations in common? Which? What holds them apart?' ('Contemporary Church, Contemporary China', in *Christian Faith and the Chinese Experience*, Lutheran World Federation and Pro Mundi Vita, Geneva and Brussels, 1974, pp. 128-129). These issues have been tackled in a number of conferences. I will make use in particular of the papers and reports of the Conference organized jointly by Pro Mundi Vita and the Lutheran World

Federation and held at Louvain 9-14 September 1974; and of the material provided at the Conference of the China Study Project of the British Council of Churches, held at Swanick, England, in May 1975.

Groups of Christians have studied China intensively, but China has so far shown no interest in Christians. The result has been a one-sided conversation. There is an obvious danger that China, precisely because it is so hard to know, will become merely a pretext for speculation or a symbol of the distant observer's aspirations. Even a visit to China is no guarantee that there will be any real grasp of the realities of Chinese life: assiduous guides shepherd the tourists everywhere and offer them glimpses of carefully selected signs of progress. Even those fortunate enough to know Chinese cannot break away from the group and speak freely with the people. The inevitable result of this veil of ignorance is that the 'perception' of China is conditioned by previous expectations. Much the same happened in Russia in the 1930s. The process was cruelly and memorably described by Malcolm Muggeridge:

> Wise old Shaw, high-minded old Barbusse, the venerable Webbs, Gide the pure in heart and Picasso the impure, down to poor little teachers, crazed clergymen and millionaires, drivelling dons and very special correspondents like Duranty, all resolved, come what might, to believe anything, however preposterous, to overlook anything, however villainous, to approve anything, however obscurantist and brutally authoritarian, in order to be able to preserve intact the confident expectation that one of the most thorough-going, ruthless and bloody tyrannies ever to exist on earth could be relied on to champion human freedom, the brotherhood of man, and all the other good liberal causes to which they had dedicated their lives (*Chronicles of Wasted Time, 1, The Green Stick*, Collins, London, 1972, pp. 275-76).

Of course it was not necessary actually to go to China to turn it into a symbol, and in one respect Muggeridge's satirical account does not apply to China: it is not liberal hopes that are thought to be vindicated but the revolutionary aspirations of the theologians of liberation discussed in Chapter 3. Gustavo Gutiérrez, for example, sees the Cultural Revolution as 'a formidable venture in turning the masses into the real makers of history' ('Theology and the Chinese Experience', in *Christian Faith and the Chinese Experience*, p. 104). Mao's maxim, 'Do not forget the class-struggle', is invoked to demonstrate that unlike Russian Marxism, with its fixed and rigid categories, Mao's version of Marxism contains a theory of 'permanent on-going criticism' which makes it superior and preferable. Gutiérrez explains: 'On the basis of this view of history as conflict he can maintain a permanent critique of every achievement and make one of the most original contributions of recent times to the dialectical method of Marxism' (*ibid.*, p. 105). However, Gutiérrez is not wholly uncritical. He concedes that 'as in every historical process, ambiguities abound, but a search for the road to follow is under way' (*ibid.*, p. 104). A footnote suggests that one of the ambiguities is the uneasiness which results from Mao's personality cult, but the matter is not pursued. Instead Gutiérrez turns with more enthusiasm to a discussion of how China compels Christians to rethink their basic assumptions. Charity, for instance, is a notion which is not easily harmonized with the imperatives of revolution. Gutiérrez is aided by the phrase of a Peruvian writer, José Maria Arguedas, who speaks of the need for a 'pure hatred' (*odio puro*). This is a sentiment 'which does not arise out of the defence of personal interests', but is used 'to express the feeling felt towards the dominating classes and their exploitation of the dispossessed' (*ibid.*, p. 106). One may legitimately wonder whether all Chinese manifestations of class-hated are quite so pure and unsullied, but such doubts do not detain Gutiérrez. He sees China through a haze of revolutionary optimism.

An even more extravagantly romantic interpretation of China is provided by Fr. Joachim Pillei, formerly professor of Theology in the Sri Lanka National Seminary. He praises Mao as 'the sage of China'. He makes a plea for indulgence: 'One should beware of immediately characterizing Mao as an atheist or a pantheist, but rather try to understand him in the cultural context in which he wrote'. The apotheosis of Mao reached new heights in the following description:

> Like a new Moses, Mao led his people from the bondage of archaism, imperialism, feudalism and capitalism. One can think of the heroic days of the 'long march' of Kiangsi. Just as on the way to the Promised Land, during the long desert trek, an ethic of right relations between God, man and nature emerged in the Ten Commandments, so too on the long and bloody trek of the Red Army, people woke up to a new socialist ethic of right relations to their fellow men and to the people (who are seen as what is sacred, as what is closest to the heart of God) ('Maoist Ethics and Judaeo-Christian Traditions', in *Christian Faith and the Chinese Experience*, p. 82).

Both Gutiérrez and Pillei can be seen as providing an answer from the third world to Mao's declaration that today 'the national liberation revolutions in Asia, Africa and Latin America are the most important forces dealing blows to imperialism'.

A rather more detailed analysis comes from two French philosophers, Guy Lardreau and Christian Jambert, who examine the parallels between early Christianity and the doctrines of Mao (*L'Ange*, Grasset, Paris, 1975). In both is found the will to absolute change, and a single-minded purity which is prepared, in Mao's phrase, 'to reject the heart of the world'. Both share in a contempt for society's conventions, and demand a willingness to break with family ties and slough off the past. 'Let the dead bury their dead' is matched by Mao's slogan, 'Down with the old ethics and up with the new'. Both share a vision of a new world with a new law. Lardreau and Jambert emphasize the role of the desert monks, who for a time constituted a mass movement. The monks strenuously sought 'perfection', and to this end ignored the distinction between commandments and counsels; Mao for his part says, 'It is not difficult for a man to do some good actions; what is difficult is to do good all his life, without ever doing evil'. Both the early monks and Mao's 'new

man' are prepared to be regarded as 'fools' by this world, know-
ing that in the light of the 'other world' towards which they
aspire, 'this world' itself is mad (parable of the Foolish Old
Man). The point of these comparisons is that both early Christianity and Maoism are instances of a *cultural* revolution which
must be sharply distinguished from an *ideological* revolution. In
an ideological revolution like the French or Russian revolutions,
one set of *ideas* is exchanged for another, but oppression has
not been abolished and it can re-appear in a new guise. A cultural revolution, on the other hand, implies new *values* and the
emergence of a new type of man. Lardreau and Jambert claim
that in the Church, the 'revolt' of the desert monks was tamed
and domesticated, and Christian language about the 'new man'
and the 'new world' was turned safely into metaphor and rheto-
ric. Thus St. Jerome and St. John Chrysostom become the
Robespierre and the Lenin who betrayed the Christian cultural
revolution.

But most Christian assessments of the new China steer a
middle course between such enthusiastic adulation and the
Manichaean view of Mao as the embodiment of the demonic.
China poses acutely the problem of how God works through the
secular. Catholics have characteristically approached this question by elaborating a theology of 'the signs of the times' in
which 'what happens' can be interpreted as an indication of
'what the Spirit is saying to the Churches' (Revelation 2:7).
Protestants have arrived at the same type of analysis by using
the World Council of Churches' idea that 'the world provides
the agenda for the Churches' and by thinking of Christ as 'Lord
of the world', and not merely 'Lord of the Church'. These theologies of the secular are easier to state than to apply. But they
both imply a constant and critical effort to distinguish between
what encourages and promotes human dignity and what is inim-
ical to it. Mao's China is an invitation to discriminate.

Whatever the motives and the methods, it is undeniable
that there has been a remarkable transformation of Chinese society, and that the lot of the peasants has been improved. Plagues
have been eliminated, rivers controlled and harnessed. Med-
ical care has advanced, and 'barefoot doctors', trained to

administer simple remedies, have improved the general level of health. Before Mao venereal disease and drug-taking were widespread in China; now they have simply vanished. Not all the experiments in agriculture have succeeded, but an efficient rationing system has ensured that the famines which periodically used to devastate China no longer have catastrophic effects. These results have been achieved by releasing the energy and dedication of the Chinese people. Self-reliance is the key to Mao's China. It leads to the voluntaristic conviction that, provided people work together, any problem can be solved. This is classically expressed in Mao's parable of the Foolish Old Man who was mocked for trying to remove the twin mountains of feudalism and imperialism. He replied: 'When I die, my sons will carry on; when they die, there will be my grandsons, and then their sons and grandsons, and so to infinity. High as they are, the mountains cannot grow any higher, and with every bit we dig, they will be that much lower'. The Foolish Old Man proved wiser than his critics.

This appeal to 'people power' has restored China's much-battered pride. In his first speech after the revolution, Mao said that China had at last 'stood up' and would never again be 'an insulted nation'. This adds a further dimension to the Chinese achievement, for although China is and remains a developing nation, its transformation has been brought about almost without outside help. Indeed, it is now in a position to give aid elsewhere. China has evolved a new model of development in which, rather than import wholesale Western industrial methods, use is made of 'intermediate technology' and small labour-intensive workshops. An ethical choice is involved here: it is more important that many should have bicycles than that few should have cars. Not that this has meant a total rejection of Western methods. China has tried, in Mao's phrase, to 'walk on two legs', combining Western technology and the talents and skills of the Chinese people. So far, so good.

Many former missionaries are prepared to concede that what the Christian missions in China attempted to achieve, and failed to achieve, has now been accomplished thanks to the regime of Chairman Mao. They argue in this way. If Marxism, in its Chinese version, has fed the hungry, transformed the lives of the oppressed and the outcasts, and brought about a more genuinely co-operative society, then it has come close to the Christian teaching that all are brothers in the one body. This positive interpretation of China can be found in a statement from the Fides News Service, published by the Vatican's Congregation for Evangelization:

> A mystique of disinterested work in the service of others; an aspiration towards justice; the exaltation of a simple and frugal life; the raising up of the peasant masses, and the merging of social classes—such are the ideals towards which the China of today is oriented. But are not the very same ideals incomparably expressed in the encyclicals *Pacem in Terris* and *Populorum Progressio*? (4 April 1973).

There is at least enough convergence to argue that some Christian values, in secularized form, have been smuggled into China through the unexpected means of Marxism.

Another 'value' some Christian commentators have detected in China is the way 'criticism' is built into every aspect of life. On this point the Chinese differ considerably from the Russians. For the Russians the Party members have become a bureaucratic class within the state. They form the *nomenklatura* which is privileged, cosseted, cut off from ordinary people, and never exposed to any kind of criticism—except in the rather drastic and arbitrary form of 'purges' directed from above. This offends against Mao's conception of Marxism. His belief that the class-struggle continues even after the revolution ensures that the Chinese Party cannot settle down and complacently enjoy the fruits of power. So Mao has restricted membership of the Party. Membership has to be earned by zeal. It brings not privileges but extra duties. Bureaucrats are despatched to the countryside to work alongside the peasants. The only tangible benefit is that Party members have better access to information. This does not mean that the Chinese CP has relinquished its 'leading role', but it does mean that it has neither the permanence nor the stable career structure of the Russian Party. Like everything else in China, it can be perpetually subjected to criticism. For Gutiérrez, this is 'one of the most original contributions to the dialectical method of Marxism'.

However, 'permanent on-going criticism' seems less admirable on closer inspection. There have been two periods in particular when criticism was allowed to flourish. The first was during the Hundred Flowers campaign of 1956-57. 'Let a hundred flowers blossom', declared Mao, 'and let a hundred schools of thought contend'. At the same time he announced a 'rectification campaign' against the 'three evils' of bureaucratism, sectarianism and subjectivism. Mao's invitation to criticize was sincere. He genuinely believed that since Marxism was the only true form of thought, it would be vindicated and confirmed if free discussion, within limits, were allowed. But it was never a policy of 'liberalization'. It had nothing to do with 'pluralism'. And it failed dismally. The criticisms that were heard were more trenchant and radical than had been anticipated. Many spoke out freely, and regretted it later. They were re-educated for their pains. They had turned into 'poisonous weeds'. The overall result was that the Hundred Flowers campaign led to a more repressive situation than had existed before. It gave way to a campaign against 'rightists', those imperfectly converted to Maoism. It is significant that Mao at this time began to think that de-Stalinization had gone dangerously far in Russia. The Hungarian uprising of 1956 was a warning of what could happen when too much freedom was conceded. The Russians were guilty of 'adventurism' and, worse still, 'revisionism'.

The second period in which criticism was encouraged was during the Cultural Revolution 1966-69. China had always had a tradition of student demonstrations, but after 1949 the tradition had lapsed. But then in 1966 the students were unleashed by Mao himself. The Red Guards were given free food and free transport and encouraged to harass Party officials and bureaucrats. They rampaged about the country, denouncing 'the old ideas, old culture, old customs and habits' of the exploiting classes and the bourgeoisie. Everywhere officials came under attack. They were denounced in poster campaigns, then dragged off to 'struggle' meetings at which they confessed their guilt and recanted. Many committed suicide. Mao's aim in releasing such unpredictable forces was to restructure the Party from below. He had more than once spoken of the dialectic power of chaos —'The more confusion the better'—which he values as the way to avoid 'bureaucratization'. Mao's way of exercising social control differs from that of Stalin. Stalin worked through the secret police; Mao works through the masses and the pressures to conform which act as a perpetual and inescapable form of group therapy. This may be considered an improvement, provided one can overlook the 'manipulation' of the masses which it involves.

Other manifestations of 'on-going criticism' have been directed against individuals once close to Mao such as Lin Piao and Teng Hsiao-ping. It seems at first blush obvious to interpret such campaigns as part of an inner-party power struggle, and quite extraordinary that the reputation of Lin Piao should have undergone such a remarkable transformation. At one time hailed as Mao's successor—he wrote the introduction to Mao's *Thoughts*—and presented as 'a glorious example' for the whole nation to follow, he was subsequently vilified as a 'bourgeois careerist, conspirator, counter-revolutionary, double-dealer, renegade and traitor'. Those nefarious tendencies had been mysteriously latent for a long time. The circumstances of Lin Piao's death in 1971 were odd, but even odder was the fact that the campaign against him did not begin until February 1974. Then, and only then, the dead Lin Piao was blamed for holding a theory of individualistic genius which went counter to the view that China's true genius was to be found in the masses. His name was linked with that of Confucius who was held responsible for many of China's traditional ills.

Teng Hsiao-ping is the latest Chinese leader to fall from grace. In 1975 he held the title of deputy prime minister and was the main spokesman on foreign affairs. In this capacity he was on hand for the visits of President Ford and West German Chancellor Schmidt, and he himself visited Paris to confer with President Giscard d'Estaing. But by March 1976 he was completely discredited and became the victim of a 'spontaneous' wall-poster campaign. He was not very illuminatingly described as a 'revisionist' and a 'capitalist roader'. The question for students of China is how far these unexpected twists of fortune represent merely a clash of personalities or how far they are the translation of a real conflict about policies to be pursued. One can dimly perceive, for example, that Teng Hsiao-ping may have interpreted Mao's injunction to 'settle down and unite' a little too literally by thinking that it was more important than the class-struggle. It is possible to argue that in each of the conflicts that have broken out, there has been a clash of principles as well as of personalities. Each time Mao has preferred mass action to the bureaucracy, political reliability to technical competence, and 'chaos' to settling down. But these are slender grounds for claiming that 'permanent on-going criticism' is Mao's principal theoretical contribution to Marxism: the criticism is too exclusively initiated from above.

Mao's contribution to Marxism lies elsewhere. He has exalted the peasants over the urbanized proletariat. This thesis has international implications in so far as he sees the 'rural areas of the world' (Asia, Africa and Latin America) as encircling the 'cities of the world' (North America and Western Europe). But it applies first of all to China which remains a peasant country. Mao defined his most significant departure from Marxist orthodoxy when he said:

> Apart from their other characteristics, China's 600 million people have two remarkable peculiarities: they are, first of all, poor, and secondly, blank. That may seem like a bad thing, but it is really a good thing. Poor people want change, want to do things, want revolution. A clean sheet of paper has no blotches, and so the newest and most beautiful words can be written on it, the newest and most beautiful pictures can be painted on it (*The Political Thought of Mao Tse-tung*, edited by Stuart Schram, Penguin Books, Harmondsworth, 1969, p. 352).

But for Marx the working-class, far from being 'blank', was capable of redeeming society as a whole because it was alienated and deprived of the fruits of its labour, but also because it was the heir to the technical accomplishments of the bourgeoisie. It was therefore able to bring the results of the industrial revolution along with it into the new state of justice and fraternity after the revolution. The notion that the working-class embody a special wisdom and insight is at the heart of Marxism. But for Mao the masses are not a source of wisdom or knowledge. They are 'blank'.

Hence the paternalism in Mao's love of the masses. His stated desire to 'learn from them' is conditional upon their accepting his direction. Left to themselves, they will get nowhere: 'The activity of the broad masses that is not oriented as it should be by a strong directing body, cannot sustain itself for long, nor develop in a right direction and lift itself to a higher level'. It follows that the exchange is somewhat unequal: 'We must sincerely learn from the masses, while we relentlessly educate them in the ideas of Mao Tse-tung', said an editorial on the fiftieth anniversary of the foundation of the Chinese Communist Party. Everything is subordinated to the Party 'line', and, as Wang Hung-wen told the tenth Party Congress in August 1973, 'Mao is the representative of the right line'.

If the virginal masses are to be 'educated' according to Mao's line, the hydra-headed and persistent remnants of the bourgeoisie are to be 're-educated' or 're-moulded'. They have been subjected to a series of vigorous campaigns of 'thought-reform'. Thought-reform is complete when the old identity is thoroughly destroyed and a new identity is substituted for it. Not all counter-revolutionaries were judged capable of thought-reform. They were eliminated. Estimates of the number of killings have varied from Chou En-lai's figure of 135,000 to ten million. Stuart Schram concludes that a 'reasonable estimate would appear to be from one to three million' (*Mao Tse-tung*, Penguin Books, 1967, p. 267). The killings were not arbitrary, at least in the sense that they had a pedagogic function: they were a way of dramatizing the class-war, and involving the peasants in the destruction of the old landlord class, for the peasants were invited to designate counter-revolutionaries and suggest suitable forms of punishment. One is familiar with

Mao's dictum that the revolution 'is not a dinner party' and aware of the crimes committed in pre-revolutionary China, but such massive terror cannot be entirely disregarded in any Christian assessment of China. The killings represent, in extreme form, Mao's tendency to consider his opponents as 'non-persons'. The poisonous weeds who deviate from the unpredictable party line can and must be uprooted, and to oppose the line is to forfeit all human rights. This can hardly be one of the 'Christian values' which have found their way incognito into China thanks to Marxism.

However, not all Christians have reached this gloomy conclusion. Workshop 3 at the Louvain Conference went a long way towards accepting Mao's idea of the continued necessity of the class-struggle, and tried to present an apologia for it:

Christians can also learn from the Chinese revolutionary rejection of the concept of universal human nature as the basis of common love. According to Mao, human nature is class-determined, and it is only after exploitation and class oppression have been overcome that a common human nature and universal love will be possible. . . . Grace and forgiveness are essentials of Christian love. To relate love to power means to affirm the active element of love—struggle. The opposite of love is not so much hatred as apathy and servility. One aspect of the Maoist concept of struggle refers to hostility towards evil and enemies. Animosity and hostility (Chinese: *hen*), such prominent features of Maoist ethics, are not antithetical to Christian love. Animosity derives from *animus* or *anima*, mind and spirit. Animosity is that which gives a dynamic or animating element to love. To love means to be animated and enlivened for struggle against all that which is opposed to love and genuine human community (*Christian Faith and the Chinese Experience*, Workshop Reports, p. 18).

It would be unfair to comment too harshly on this anthology piece of Orwellian 'newspeak'. Workshop 5 at Louvain had a greater sense of nuances. It tried to balance its sympathy for

China with a recognition of the dangers to which total social control could lead:

> There are two aspects to any form of organization: social control by authority, and participation in organizational processes by those united under authority. The high degree of organization in the new China involves an extremely deep penetration of political authority into the fabric of Chinese society. It also involves an unprecedented opportunity for the Chinese masses to participate in the political process. There is thus danger as well as opportunity in the tightly-knit organization of Chinese society. The deep penetration of political authority into social life presents the danger of totalitarian control; the degree of popular participation offers the opportunity of a freedom in which hundreds of millions of people can work together for the good of all (*ibid.*, p. 24).

However, Workshop 5 did not answer the central question: does the totalitarian danger prevail over the opportunity for participation? It is no doubt true that Mao did not want to produce a nation of mechanized ants, but his 'model' of society owed a great deal to his military experience. The idea of 'brigades' had been extended to work-teams in the fields and factories. But the military model permits 'initiative' only within the narrow boundaries prescribed from above.

What is euphemistically called 'the deep penetration of the political authority into social life' means in practice the attempt at complete social control. The process of indoctrination starts in the nursery where there are already classes in Maoist thought. The children learn by 'singing songs and telling stories with revolutionary content' (Ruth Sidel, *Women and Child Care in China*, Hill and Wang, 1972/Sheldon Press, London, 1974, p. 120). Ruth Sidel describes a typical kindergarten scene in which a group of five-year-old dancers sing a popular song on the theme 'It is ridiculous to have two Chinas: we are determined to liberate Taiwan'. Accompanied by a teacher playing the accordion, 'with fierce expressions on their faces and fists raised in revolutionary determination, the children sing: "The poor people of the world must win victories" ' (*ibid.*, p. 129). By the time they have finished kindergarten, the children can read simple sentences such as 'Long live Chairman Mao'. The filial piety which marked the old China has been transformed into fil-ial piety towards Mao who has been increasingly presented as all-wise, all-knowing, all-powerful and ever solicitous for his people. Rumours of death, illness or enforced retirement could undermine faith in Mao.

This is the most disquieting aspect of the new China. The cult of Mao has been pushed to quite extraordinary lengths. It is so thorough-going and all-embracing that it makes Stalin's efforts to promote his personality cult look botched and ama-teurish by comparison. Mao has acquired all the characteristics of a religious leader. He is credited with an infallibility no Pope ever claimed. His earlier works are carefully re-written to elimi-nate the impression that he ever made a mistake or changed his mind (which he has plainly done). A quotation from Mao can be used to settle an argument. There are no limits set to the uni-versal and absolute validity of Mao's thought. A typical state-ment says of him:

What I call 'belief' means believing in Mao's thought; moreover, this belief must be steadfast and immovable. In the course of China's revolutionary struggles and socialist construction, vast practical experience has demonstrated that Mao Tse-tung's thought is the only correct thought. It is the incarnation of Marxism-Leninism in China; it is the symbol of truth. Therefore, if a person at any time what-ever, in any place whatever, regarding any question what-ever, manifests a wavering in his attitude towards Mao Tse-tung's thought, no matter if this wavering is only mo-mentary and slight, it means in reality that the waverer departs from Marxist-Leninist truth and will lose his bear-ings and commit political errors. So we must follow Chair-man Mao steadfastly and eternally! Forward, following a hundred per cent and without the slightest reservation the way of Mao Tse-tung! (Liu Tzu-chi in 1959, quoted in Schram, *Mao Tse-tung*, p. 326).

The cult of Mao also had the marks of religious ritual. The parades and processions, the public confessions and recantations, the wall posters, the chanting of slogans while The Little Red Book is held aloft, were all reminiscent of religious ritual. The sight of Mao evoked feelings akin to religious fervor. *The Peking Review* reported in 1966: 'When Chairman Mao drove past the ranks of the revolutionary teachers and students . . . many students quickly opened their copies of *Quotations from Chairman Mao* and wrote the same words on the flyleaf: "At 1:10 p.m. on October 18, the most, most happy and the most, most unforgettable moment of my life, I saw Chairman Mao, the never-setting red sun" '. It is difficult to see how an *ersatz* this-wordly religion, backed up by tremendous physical and psychological pressures to conform, can justly be described as 'liberating' and a foreshadowing of the Kingdom of God on earth.

There was irony in the way Mao, having destroyed so much of the old China, became himself the object of new superstitions. His death on 9 September 1976 made him a still more sacred and untouchable figure, for Mao could not possibly transmit his wisdom and his authority since they were based, it was always claimed, on his vast and unique experience of leadership. There was no easy apostolic succession. The first concern of his successor, Hua Kuo-feng, was to secure a monopoly of the editing and interpretation of the works of Mao, and to oust his widow and other Shanghai 'radicals'. The shadow of Mao's authority lingers after him. Thus what began as a critical method has been turned into a manipulative ideology. As Péguy said: *Tout commence en mystique et finit en politique.* And Christians may be forgiven for thinking that superstition rushes in to fill the void left where faith is absent, and that the cult of Mao makes a statement about man's need for the absolute which is formally denied in contemporary China. That would be the strangest of the divine disguises.

The Chinese have always believed that China was 'the central country', and that its experience had an exemplary and universal value; Mao has clothed this theme in Marxist language. But if one recognizes the uniqueness of China, one also has to add that the Chinese model of development cannot be exported elsewhere in the third world without considerable modification. Third world countries can learn a lot from China about self-reliance and intermediate technology; but they have their own cultural traditions which must be respected. This is also the lesson which 'the China experience' teaches Christian missionaries: they will fail if they act as the agents of cultural imperialism. If Christians feel judged by China, they have not forfeited the right to judge the China of Mao and wonder at the price that has been paid for its undoubted achievements. God may be 'at work in China', but China impoverishes itself by subordinating the individual so completely to the collectivity and shutting off the horizon of transcendence. For centuries, China rightly complained of being misunderstood. The balance is not now adjusted by misunderstanding Christianity. Mao's parable of the Foolish Old Man has its parallel in the Gospels which also speak of moving mountains. The coincidence has sometimes been used to contrast reliance on human effort with trusting to prayer. Christians will want to refuse that dichotomy, insisting that prayer is not an escape but a commitment and that God and man are not in competition. Until that misunderstanding is overcome, China will remain an ambivalent sign.

6
The Sincerity
of the Euro-Communists

In bringing the story of Christians and Marxists up to the present, we are brought face to face with a paradox: at the very moment that some Christians are discovering the subversive potential of the Gospel and urging the need for revolution, official Communist Parties in Western Europe are embarrassed by talk of revolution, have little interest in subversion, and declare their faith in democracy and 'the peaceful transition to socialism'. It is as though the two groups were moving in opposite directions, up and down Jacob's ladder: down comes Enrico Berlinguer, speaking soothingly of the *compromesso storico* or alliance with Christian Democrats, while up goes Giulio Girardi, advocating a revolutionary transformation of society which Berlinguer has rejected or postponed. There is an ironical contrast between the moderate and reasonable language of the 'Euro-Communists' and the aggressive language of Christian Marxists. One of them, Neil Middleton, rewrites the text of John 14:6 so that it now reads: 'I am the way, the truth and the revolution'. By way of explanation, he adds: 'For revolution, not necessarily bloody, is life—it is the indication that life is there' (*The Language of Christian Revolution*, Sheed and Ward, 1968, p. 129). Nothing could be further from the thoughts of the Euro-Communists, at least in their official public utterances. The leader of the French Communists, Georges Marchais, has said that 'the desire to work for democratic changes is a sufficient condition for membership' (of the Communist Party). Meanwhile, in those parts of the world where the Communists actually hold power, the 'revolution', now safely in the past, is invoked as the legitimating cover for distinctly undemocratic policies. But so long as it remains somewhere in the future, 'revolution' can continue to act as a powerful and imaginative symbol of hope, a speeded up and apocalyptic version of the myth of progress. The nineteenth century believed in progress; the impatient twentieth century needs revolution.

The piquant oddity of these contrasts provides further evidence of how slippery language can be, and prompts a whole cluster of questions. But for the moment they can be reduced to one. Has Marxism—in the form it is now taking in Western Communist Parties—really changed in a fundamental way? Has 'revisionism' bitten deeply into them, and is their announced conversion to democracy sincere? Do they exemplify Girardi's distinction between 'the Marxism of institutions' and 'human Marxism'?

Some assessments of Euro-Communism simply deny that there has been any real change. Such adjustments as have been made are superficial and merely 'cosmetic'. They are designed to reassure and win over the mass electorate in Italy, France and eventually Spain. The verbal concessions are a deceptive camouflage, a tactic of *reculer pour mieux sauter*. In this analysis the Vatican—to judge by the statements of the Italian Episcopal Conference—is in substantial agreement with Dr. Henry Kissinger. Speaking at Boston on 11 March 1976, the American Secretary of State said:

> Whether some of the Communist parties in Western Europe are independent of Moscow cannot be determined when their electoral self-interest so overwhelmingly coincides with their claims. . . . Their internal procedures, their Leninist principles and dogmas, remain the antithesis of democratic parties. And were they to gain power, they would do so after having advocated for decades programs and values detrimental to our traditional ties.

Dr. Kissinger was much criticized for 'interfering in the internal affairs' of the countries concerned. It would have been more relevant to point out that his verdict would have been more convincing if it were presented as the conclusion of an argument rather than its premise.

One can fill in the missing steps of the argument by using the distinctions developed by Professor Ronald Tiersky (*French Communism, 1920-1972*, Columbia University Press, New York, 1974). What he says of the French CP applies also to other countries where the Party has a reasonable expectation of coming to power by the ballot box. For Tiersky, the French CP has four 'faces' and sees itself in four 'roles'. Sometimes it appears as the Marxist revolutionary vanguard, which embodies the destiny and the privileged grasp of the movement of history which is attributed to the working-class: in this role, it is not one party among others so much as 'history made conscious', and its ultimate victory is not in doubt. But secondly, it can present itself as a sort of 'counter-culture', with its own schools, press, life-style and values: in this role it is, as it were, camping out in the uncongenial context of doomed capitalism. Sometimes a third function can come to the fore: the Party acts as 'the people's tribune', standing up for the little man against oppression and acting as the champion of the under-privileged —most of its deservedly popular 'one-issue' campaigns are based on this role. Finally, the Communist Party can see itself as a mass party, seeking the free adherence of the electorate, and therefore as potentially a responsible 'party of government'. In the last decade the fourth function has taken over from the first: the desire to emerge from the ghetto and exercise power in government predominates over the historical role of embodying working-class insights into the meaning of history. A natural consequence is that the more dogmatic aspects of Marxism, which belong to the first role, are toned down and are replaced by a more flexible and pragmatic approach which is commanded by electoral ambitions. The recent history of the French CP illustrates this process at work.

Piece by piece, it has dismantled important elements in Marxist theory. The French CP long ago abandoned the hope or the expectation of coming to power by violent revolution. The new 'line' is that the appropriate strategy for France is to create a broadly based movement of the left, open also to non-

Communists and particularly to Catholics. This would lead to 'the peaceful transition to socialism', but in the agreement with the Socialist Party known as *le programme commun*, even 'the peaceful transition to socialism' has given way to the misty concept of 'advanced democracy'. There is obviously—from the point of view of the CP itself—a grave danger of doctrinal dilution involved in becoming a mass party, and Georges Marchais is not unaware of this problem:

> We must realize that after the presidential elections, hundreds of thousands of people want to participate in our activity. . . . Obviously they do not all have a clear vision of our strategy and of the final objectives of the party. But this cannot be an insurmountable obstacle to their membership (*Cahiers du Communisme*, November 1974, p. 55).

Marchais is here attempting to reassure both the inner-Party elite, who *are* endowed with the 'clear vision of our strategy and of the final objectives of the Party', and at the same time potential supporters who have not (or not yet) perceived the vision. The dilemma—mass or elite—is solved in principle by envisaging two levels of membership.

But more attention has been devoted to reassuring the sceptical mass public than to consoling the perturbed Party activists. The French CP has begun to talk a new language. In alliance with the Socialist Party it has undertaken to acknowledge the role of opposition parties in any future regime ('pluralism'), and declared that it would accept the rules of French parliamentary procedure and retire if defeated at the polls ('*alternance*'). These are important concessions. But at their Twenty-Second Party Congress held at Ile-Saint-Denis in February 1976, the French Communists went further still and unanimously endorsed the abandonment of 'the dictatorship of the proletariat'. In Lenin the term meant that the power seized at the revolution would then be turned against those who had previously exercised it. Marchais went on French television to explain how 'outmoded' (*dépassé*) was this idea. It had been, he suggested, 'outgrown, as one outgrows a suit of clothes'. But a more powerful reason for abandoning it without any deep sense of loss was that it had been corrupted beyond redemption: in practice 'the dictatorship of the proletariat' had come to mean 'the dictatorship of the party' or, in certain cases, of the individual who controlled the party. Some hard-line Communists regretted the loss of a slogan which they had repeated for so many years, but after a brief flurry of rueful letters in *Humanité*, no more was heard from them.

Special attention has been paid to Catholics. On 10 June 1976, M. Marchais devoted the whole of a ninety-minute speech to their reassurance. Its main theme was that collaboration was possible, since 'men are not divided into those who believe in heaven and those who do not'. In particular, he gave the following assurance: 'We will never declare war on religion. . . . We have, for example, no taste for anti-religious exhibitions, which in our time run the risk of being no more than a masquerade in poor taste'. Marchais was evidently thinking of the atheist museum in Kiev, where one can learn how the priests simulated the miracle of the 'Weeping Virgin' by trickery. There followed a long list of rights which would be guaranteed to the Church: liberty of conscience, religious education, freedom of worship, and the Church would be able to own property, train its own clergy, possess publishing houses. In short, in the future socialist regime (Marchais did not specify whether he was speaking of 'advanced democracy' or of some later stage of development), the state would be neutral. It would be 'neither atheist nor Christian'.

Taken at their face-value, these changes are remarkable. They would mean that the French CP has accepted 'the long march through democratic institutions' and now advocates tolerance for Christians. But it was not enough for the French Communists to adopt a more reasonable and amenable tone of voice. The great weakness of their new positions was that they seemed incredible in the light of previous utterances. What guarantees were there that the promises would be kept? The French CP knew that one of the principal reasons it aroused mistrust was its history of dependence—often humiliating dependence—on the Soviet Union. If, then, its appeal to a mass public were to succeed, it would have to risk annoying the Soviet Union. It would have to show that it was not merely a puppet on a Moscow string.

The French CP has worked hard at upsetting the Russians. In November 1975, it reached an agreement with the Italian CP, judged by Moscow to be the most 'revisionist' and unreliable of Western Parties. After a film on French television had given a detailed account of life in Soviet labour camps, and been dismissed by *Pravda* as a 'gross fake', the French CP challenged the Russians formally to deny the existence of such camps. 'When one loves liberty in Paris', said Marchais grandly, 'one must love it elsewhere, whatever the country'. With its new-found interest in human rights, the French CP also took up the case of Leonid Plyushch, the interned Soviet mathematician. Relations became so strained that M. Marchais could not even summon the energy to go to Moscow for the Twenty-Fifth Congress in February 1976, where he would have heard his heretical views denounced by Mr. Brezhnev. The main charge against him and the Euro-Communists generally is that they have abandoned the sacrosanct principle of 'international working-class solidarity', which in practice means subordination to the line propounded by Moscow. The French and Italian CPs have not only declared that there are different roads to socialism, but also that there are no pre-existent 'models' of the forthcoming socialist society. Russia ceases to be the Communist Mecca.

Moreover, the French CP has set its intellectuals the task of rewriting history. In his book *Le Phénomène Stalinien* Jean Elleinstein is not content with the usual line which attributes Stalin's aberrations to the 'personality cult'. What happened in Soviet Russia, says Elleinstein, can be explained by the special circumstances of that huge country: the absence of democratic traditions, the feudal social structure, the international and civil war which preceded and followed the revolution. Stalin's perversion of Marxism was essentially that he turned a flexible response into a dogmatic system. Elleinstein's work can be seen as an attempt to cope with awkward facts which, after Solzhenitsyn, it is impossible to deny; but the main point of his laborious explanations is that in France Communism would build on French democratic traditions and consequently would take on a different character.

'It will be different in France' has become a major theme of Georges Marchais. After his assurances to Christians on 10 June 1976, he envisaged and answered the obvious objection:

> People say to us: but what you propose is quite different from what happens in socialist countries today. They are right! It will be different! We follow our own way, the way which fits in with the conditions of our time and our country (*Le Monde*, 12 June 1976).

However, such ringing declarations about some hypothetical future carry less weight when one contemplates the Communist Party as it is at present constituted. Its commitment to democracy has not meant that it allows democracy to flourish in its own ranks. It is truly astonishing that no voices were raised at the Party Congress to complain of the dropping of 'the dictatorship of the proletariat'. Indeed, the 1,522 delegates at Ile-Saint-Denis voted unanimously for all the resolutions and reports put before them, and elected unanimously all the members of the central committee. This remarkable show of unanimity did not come about by accident. The suppression of dissent within the Party is evidence of the unreformed habits of mind which still prevail. It is hard to see how, at some future date, 'democracy' can be suddenly expected to burgeon without any preliminary cultivation.

But there are other reasons for not accepting at face-value the sincerity of the conversion to democracy of the Euro-Communists. Although the current emphasis is on a 'soft line' intended to reassure potential voters, the role of revolutionary *avant-garde* has not been abandoned, and all the guarantees given on the peaceful conquest of power, the preservation of democratic liberties, the pluralism of political parties, the acceptance of defeat at the polls (should it come about) are accompanied by disquieting nuances which qualify these apparent concessions. There has been no relaxation of the class-war.

Georges Marchais wrote: 'The only class that is able to provide the basis of a union against big capitalism is the working-class. It remains the essential force of the revolutionary struggle' (*Le Parti Communiste Propose*, November 1974, p. 73). In speaking of the plurality of political parties, Marchais does not use the obvious example to hand of the Scandinavian or Western European democracies; instead he uses the model of the Eastern European Communist countries where, he appears to believe, pluralism is in good health (*Le Défi Démocratique*, Grasset, 1973, pp. 127-128). As for '*alternance*'—the acceptance of defeat at the polls—the substance of this concession is somewhat eroded by the fact that opposition parties are envisaged as existing only within 'the new framework of legality' which will be set up. There are proposals for 'electoral reform' which will make a clear-cut opposition victory unlikely. And if all else fails, there is in reserve the convenient strand of theory according to which a left-wing victory might well provoke a right-wing reaction, which, regrettably but inevitably, would have to be dealt with by force.

But the most fundamental point of all is that the Communist Party, despite its hopes of an electoral victory, *does not rest its case on a mandate received from a majority*; its right to rule is derived from elsewhere, from its metaphysical claim to be the party which embodies the aspirations of the working-class. Marchais explains:

> The workers, all the democrats, must have at their disposal a fighting party, determined, clear-sighted and effective. This party is the Communist Party. It can and does play the role of vanguard of the working class and the people, because it is the party of the class that is most interested in the transformation of society, the working class; because it bases its action on a revolutionary theory that is constantly enriched with new conclusions drawn from experience; because it has rules of unity that assure its unity of action (*Le Parti Communiste Propose*, p. 84).

This over-riding conviction determines how the French CP

would treat its allies and its opponents. Even though it can form an alliance with the Socialists and extend a friendly hand to Catholics, it has not abandoned the idea that it has a leading role to play. Irrespective of its voting strength, it remains *the* party of the left, pre-destined to its leading role by the laws of history themselves. This truth abides 'objectively', no matter how many votes are cast against the Party, and the anti-Communist votes are attributed to 'brain-washing', 'intimidation', 'socialization into the system', or just plain 'alienation'. This became clear in Portugal, and caused embarrassment to the French and Italian CPs. The leader of the Portuguese CP, Alvaro Cunhal, declared that there would be 'no parliament in Portugal', and that votes cast against those who are 'objectively' on the side of freedom and justice do not count and can be ignored (Interview with Orlana Fallaci, in *L'Europeo*, Milan, 13 June 1975). There is no need of an 'arithmetical majority' when destiny is on one's side.

There can be no substantial change in Marxism so long as the doctrine of the historic mission of the working-class, interpreted by the Communist Party alone, remains so central. The Italian CP stresses this theme just as much as the French CP. The Italian Communists differ from the French in three principal ways: they are not dependent on the Socialist Party for the prospect of eventual electoral success; they had an honorable record of struggling against Fascism during the long rule of Mussolini—and it is tempting to suppose that 'anti-Fascists' are pro-democrat; the years of Christian Democratic rule since the war have not been glorious, and the Communists appear as the only possible opposition force with any chance of success. Moreover, the Italian Communists can boast a longer record of independent thinking. The man usually credited with being the founder of the Party, Antonio Gramsci, was one of the few truly original Marxist thinkers. His principal concern was that workers should run their own factories through workers' councils; and he also believed that the cultural preparation of the masses for revolution was a condition of its success in depth, and that it was not enough for an elite to seize and exercise power. Gramsci required considerable intellectual agility to rec-

oncile these convictions with Leninist practice, for Lenin had come to power with the aid of a determined minority in a distinctly 'opportunist manner', the 'cultural preparation of the Russian people for the revolution' barely existed, and the 'spontaneous' workers' soviets had been swiftly dissolved. Gramsci fought his way out of the contradiction by conceding the need for discipline and necessarily simplified slogans.

The Italian CP is still struggling with these problems. Like its founder, it does not think of itself as a force external to the working-class, an authoritarian imposition from above, but rather as 'the working-class become conscious', the articulate spokesman on behalf of a not fully articulate working-class. There is an obvious danger that this role may lead the Party to substitute itself for the working-class. And like the French CP, the Italian CP remains authoritarian internally. When Enrico Berlinguer spoke in favor of 'democracy' and 'pluralism' at the twenty-fifth Congress of the Russian Communist Party in February 1976, the context clearly indicated that 'democracy' referred not to any internal debate within a given party but to civil rights, and 'pluralism' meant accepting differences between Communist Parties rather than toleration of a political opposition. To differ from Moscow is admirable, but it cannot alone be used as evidence of the democratic temper. Albania differs from Moscow. So does China.

The siren voices of the Euro-Communists should not lull us into the belief that they have forgotten or abandoned their first and principal function which is to embody the meaning of history. They continue to claim privileged access to what Marx called 'the answer to the riddle of history'. Marxism, therefore, remains an *ideology*. The implications of this statement for Christian-Marxist relations will be examined in the next chapter.

7
Ideology
and Incompatibility

Marxism is an ideology. 'Ideology' is an innocent-sounding word, and it can be used neutrally or pejoratively. It can be purely descriptive or it can enshrine a value-judgment. I use the term in its pejorative sense as a system of self-justification which runs well beyond the available evidence, takes on the character of a faith while claiming to be a science, and characteristically dismisses opponents as deluded or motivated only by class-interest. 'The social function of ideologies', writes Patrick Corbett, 'is to condition men intellectually to obedience' (*Ideologies,* Hutchinson, London 1965, p. 57). Like all self-justifying systems, an ideology beguiles its adepts, argues in a circular manner, and, once it has been embraced, the world does indeed begin to look different. The most difficult question facing those who call themselves Christian Marxists is whether they can succeed in making critical distinctions within the ideology of Marxism.

The Marxist ideology is said to be scientific, but this term involves a gross misuse of language. Too many facts have to be ignored for it to be even remotely plausible. The neat division into exploiters and exploited, though excellent as a slogan, does not correspond to the sociological facts of Western and North American societies. The 'affluent worker', whose standard of living rises as capitalist activity develops and who increasingly looks for some form of participation in management, is not allowed for in Marxist theory. The modifications introduced into capitalism to check its abuses and injustices have been such that neo-capitalism no longer resembles the *laissez-faire* jungle denounced by Marx and Leo XIII in *Rerum Novarum*. No modern state refuses some degree of intervention in the free play of market forces. Technological innovations, particularly automation, and changed conditions of work have transformed the debate on 'alienation'. Even in Latin America, the simple division into 'exploiters' and 'exploited' will not do, since it leaves out of account the 'marginalized' Indians, the original inhabitants of the sub-continent, who are the victims of 'internal colonization' at the expense of the Europeanized working-class. But no number of contrary facts or falsified predictions can disturb the Marxist once he has put on the spectacles which filter and transform common experience. His conviction is based on other grounds. It depends on ideology.

In Communist societies the ideology can be seen at work. Its function is to screen out disturbing ideas or disagreeable facts or anything that would upset the *status quo*. The complete control of the mass media makes this process possible, limited only by the scepticism of the citizens. But the regime leaves nothing to chance. For example, a new set of regulations governing the censorship of Catholic publications in Poland, made public thanks to an indiscretion in April 1976, forbade in particular any items 'crediting the Church with a positive role in the national and political arena', and 'any mention whatsoever of ideological pluralism, or value-judgments on ideologies currently existing in Poland, or assessments of their value made by pointing to the superiority of one over the other' (*Documentation Catholique*, 4 July 1976). Such terrified nervousness in the face of ideas is evidence of deep insecurity. When Mr. Brezhnev and Mr. Gierek speak of 'strengthening the battle on the ideological front', they seem to be unaware that they are using 'ideology' precisely in the sense intended by Marx when he denounced capitalist societies: it provides the justification for a kind of 'dynamic conservatism' in which nothing really changes. And by another Orwellian twist of language, this maintenance of the *status quo* is called 'progressive' or even 'revolutionary'.

Graver still, Marxism has so far acted as a *total* ideology. This can be seen most clearly in its treatment of religion, in theory and in practice. It is sometimes suggested that Christians over-estimate their own importance, and use the treatment of religion as a yardstick to judge Marxism when other criteria might be more important. Yet the treatment of religion by Marxists is an important indicator of the nature of Marxism. If they could contrive, theoretically and practically, to tolerate Christianity even as a private option, then we would know that Marxism had ceased to be a total *Weltanschauung,* an all-embracing ideology, and had modestly reduced itself to the level of a technique for the ordering of society, without any meta-physical pretensions. But nowhere has Marxism managed to achieve this scaling down of its universalist claims. For all the talk of 'outstretched hands' and strategic alliances, for all the appeals to Christians to 'join in the struggle', no one has ever suggested that there is any modification of the traditional Marxist view of religion. The treatment proposed may differ, but the theory behind it does not. Now the step from a total, all-embracing world-view to totalitarianism is a short one. Where 'politics is in command', to use Mao's phrase, no aspect of human life ever escapes, except by accident, the vast project of human engineering. Religion, in so far as it offers an alternative account of man, his value and his destiny, will necessarily be thought of as a rival, a competitor, a disturbing element in the self-contained project. Historically, this is what we find to be the case. The judgment is not an *a priori* one. While it may be theoretically possible to separate Marxism as 'analysis' from Marxism as a total ideology, this is not a distinction which operates in practice.

Moreover, there is a philosophical reason why the chances of making such a distinction are slender. Despite his attempt to 'stand Hegel on his head', Marx borrowed much from his pre-decessor. The permanent Hegelian influence on Marx has been studied by Charles Taylor in his *Hegel* (Cambridge University Press, 1975). Although for Marx the driving power of history is no longer Spirit whose essence is rational necessity, dialectical materialism, which takes on this role, continues to be envisaged as necessary and inevitable. Secondly, Marx posits a stage, after the revolution, when there will be an end to all alienations, when, in short, history will have ceased. The absolute quality of

Marxist ideology has its roots in this utopian claim. Marx begins with an attack on Enlightenment optimism, and then proceeds to rehabilitate Enlightenment optimism. The clumsy old raft turns over, and a different side of the same stuff comes uppermost. Marxism fails, and necessarily fails, because of the totalitarian pretentiousness of its intellectual claims. 'I believe', writes Taylor, 'that the root cause of its inadequacy is that it isn't true; its solution is based on an illusion about the human condition. The promise that it holds out of complete reconciliation of man to other men, his creation of himself, all in one act, is unfulfillable' (*From Culture to Revolution*, edited by Terry Eagleton and Brian Wicker, Sheed and Ward, 1968, p. 153). It is this unjustified ideological optimism which enables Marxists to remain blind to the contradictions between their theory and practice. And the hostility to religion can be traced to the same cause, for the continued existence of religion in Communist society is clear evidence that all alienations have not yet been overcome.

Even in the speech in which he called upon Christians to join in the struggle and offered assurances of benign treatment, Georges Marchais continued to insist that religion 'is for us a complex reflection in human consciousness of a world of oppression which calls forth another, happier world' (10 June 76). The remark should be interpreted in the light of his earlier observation that 'the end of alienation will mark the end of religious ideology, which is its reflection' (Interview in *La Croix*, 19 November 1970). For *atheism is essential to Marxism.* Even the revisionist Czech philosopher Gardavsky holds on to this. Atheism is essential, he writes, because without it 'both Marx's plan for a "total man" and his concept of communism are equally inconceivable' (*God Is Not Yet Dead,* p. 157). Gardavsky's position is worth considering in some detail because, like Marchais and unlike most Marxist thinkers, he claims to 'take religion seriously'. Gardavsky takes the trouble to define the special quality of Marxist atheism, and he insists on the most rigorous standards. Marxist atheism, he says, should not be confused with the *naive* atheism of the Enlightenment which enthroned reason in theory and generated irrationality and brutality in practice. Nor should it be confused with *practical* atheism which never asks any serious questions. Nor with *conform-ist* atheism which, in Communist countries, is a necessary job qualification. Nor with *anti-clerical* atheism which simply lets the churches know what their next adaptive move should be. Nor with *abstract humanist* atheism which is the tender-minded resolution of a personal crisis of faith, a sort of lapsed theism. Marxist atheism differs from these fumbling precursors in that it is systematic, total and radical, and understands that which it rejects. Marxist atheism, we are told, 'goes beyond religion, for it includes all the different historical phases in the development and criticism of Christianity and *takes them over*' (p. 157). Believers are doomed survivors from a discredited pre-history. They can be tolerated in socialist society, but only in a provisional way. Their existence, in fact, reminds the Marxists of their unfinished business. 'The rise or fall of religiosity', writes Gardavsky, 'acts as a sort of barometer by which he (the Marxist atheist) can judge the success or the failure of his political commitment to the task of emancipating his fellow men' (*ibid.*, p. 172). So long as religion survives, he has work to do. One should not forget, he explains, that 'ideological uniformity takes time' (p. 154). God is not yet dead, but he soon will be.

The persistence of religion means a gap in the system of total social control. Gardavsky's most revealing remark is that the original idea of the Czech Communists was that 'a world without God would be clearer and easier to control' (p. 153).

The incompatibility between Marxism and Christianity could hardly be stated more clearly. No subtlety of dialectic can sweep it away. On this point Marxists seem to be more clear-sighted than Christians. In an interview, the minister responsible for religious affairs in Poland, Kazimierz Kakol, was asked whether one could be 'both a member of the Communist Party and of the Church'? He replied:

I think not. Membership in the Party does not merely consist in paying dues: it is an ideological commitment. If the basis of the Party is dialectical materialism, then one cannot be both a materialist and a believer in God. . . . But there are some situations that the Party doesn't look at in rigid terms. For instance, a peasant who enters the Party but who has not looked into its entire philosophical base and remains a church-goer might be judged differently from an intellectual. But a person of a certain level of intellectual development must make a choice (Interview with Kazimierz Kakol, *Newsweek*, 10 February 1975).

The question which Christian Marxists have to face is simple enough: Is Marxism, as Kazimierz Kakol insists, an *ideological commitment* (which includes atheism) or is it not? Will the advent of socialism, as even Georges Marchais, the Euro-Communist, admits, mean 'the end of religious ideology'?

These questions are either obfuscated or eluded by Christian Marxists. In February 1976 a group of sixty 'committed Christians' who had made 'the socialist option' objected most strongly to a statement by Bishop Gabriel Matagrin of Grenoble who had formulated the objections to Marxism with great trenchancy. Matagrin's statement is worth quoting at some length:

The popes have never ceased to condemn capitalism in all its forms: the subordination of the spiritual life to consumption, of consumption to production, and of production to money. But, from Leo XIII to Paul VI, they have also never ceased to condemn Communism, denouncing it as a remedy worse than the evil it seeks to cure. Marxism has not really separated itself from the philosophy of economic liberalism which defines man in the first instance in terms of production and consumption, and the surest proof of this is the fact that it thinks it has found in the organization of production the cause of the fundamental alienation which, if suppressed, would set man free. Ideological materialism confines man within purely earthly horizons, and in its atheism fails to recognize the most essential characteristic of man, his desire for God. This failure to recognize that the human person is an absolute means that Communism is unable either to establish in theory or guarantee in practice man's essential freedom and the other freedoms that de-

volve from it. The theory of the class struggle, considered
as a determining factor in historical progress, encloses humanity in an infernal cycle of violence.

The drama of the contemporary world lies in the fact that
the oppressed everywhere imagine they have found the way
to liberation within a framework which has never produced
anything but totalitarianism. Emmanuel Mounier's judgment is still relevant: Marxism 'formulates the tensions of
a dying civilization'. But at the same time it obscures the
issue. . . . What is at stake is the future of freedom. Con-
fronted with an increasing number of totalitarian regimes,
both of the right and of the left, will the best have the spiritual strength to defend, preserve and foster the freedom
which has been so dearly won by democracy? ('Catholics
and Communism in France', in *The Tablet*, 7 February
1976, pp. 132-133).

The 'committed Christians' tried two lines of reply to this attack. The first was to say that it hardened their positions, and
that there was great diversity among them which Bishop Matagrin had unaccountably overlooked: 'Some of us are definitely
Marxist, according to an interpretation of Marxism judged to
be in accord with the faith; some are still searching; some have
accepted certain aspects of Marxism; and some, finally, are not
themselves Marxists, but collaborate with Marxists in the political struggle' (*The Tablet*, 14 February 1976). These are all very
different positions, it is true, which should not be yoked together; but to point this out is not an answer to the Bishop's
questions which were directly addressed to the first category,
those who have claim to have made a synthesis between Christianity and Marxism. The second tactic was to accuse Bishop
Matagrin of constantly confusing 'Marxism as a philosophy, the
Marxist method of analyzing society, revolutionary *praxis*,
Communism and totalitarianism'. But the connection between
these admittedly different ideas is not something invented by the
Bishop of Grenoble: it is constantly made in the Marxist texts
and is borne out by observation. If the connection made is an il-

legitimate one, the onus of proof lies upon the Christian Marxists. They have to show, and not merely to assert, that the 'philosophy' is *in practice* separable from the analysis of society, and that Communism is *in practice* separable from totalitarianism. So far these tasks have not been accomplished.

Other Marxist Christians try another tack. They say that the Communist Parties, both in and out of power, have discredited and betrayed authentic Marxism. The Communist Parties are discounted because they have replaced the capitalism of the bosses by state capitalism and because they have turned Marxism into an opportunist ideology designed to keep them in power. This judgment does credit to their perceptiveness, but it also leaves them caught in a dilemma. For outside the Communist Party, the banner of Marxism is upheld by small splinter groups such as the International Socialists and the International Marxist Group which quarrel fiercely among themselves. Moreover, the Marxist sects have no conception of dialogue with Christians, and console themselves for their inefficacy by being even more fiercely dogmatic than the Communist Parties. Lacking any broadly based support among the working-classes they purport to represent, they are left with a touching but unfounded faith in their own destiny. Christian Marxists can hardly expect to find a home among the dissident Marxists to the left of the Communist Party. In any case, Marxism outside the Communist Party is condemned to remain on the drawing board. Christian Marxists, who claim to reject all 'idealism' and exalt 'praxis', are entrapped in this dilemma: either they support the Communist Party, but in the process they have to compromise with a corrupted version of Marxism: or they reject it, and pin their hopes on a 'critical Marxism' which so far has nothing to show except volumes of theorizing.

This no doubt accounts for the air of unreality which envelops much of the language of the Christian Left. By way of illustration, I will give two examples of the way Christian Marxists attempt to argue their case. We have already seen the argument that Christianity and Marxism are not and cannot be incompatible because they operate on different levels. In Gutiérrez this argument depends upon the premise that Marxism is a 'science', and therefore can no more conflict with Christianity than can biology. Fr. Laurence Bright, O.P., suggests an interesting variation of the 'two levels' argument in which Marxism provides that 'detailed analysis and strategy' which Christianity lacks:

> If Christianity is a revolutionary movement rather than a belief in abstract doctrinal statements, if it is concerned with change in man's actual situation, with political ways of breaking down unjust divisions between men, then it is at least not incompatible with Marxism in a broad sense. . . . We have to use the forms of institution worked out by contemporary secular thinking in order to make Christian ideals a reality in the world.

One could hardly find a clearer example of the way Christianity is first operated upon in order to make synthesis possible. Secondly, Fr. Bright is perfectly clear on which factor is in the end determining:

> A Christian has to recognize, first of all, that in itself Christianity is not enough; it can only be realized in a practical way through detailed analysis and strategy. But the detailed analysis and strategy which Marxism provides must then be judged, however critically, in its own terms; the Christian who accepts some form of Marxism judges it as a Marxist, not specifically as a Christian (*What Kind of Revolution?* Edited by James Klugmann and Paul Oestreicher, Panther Books, London, 1968, pp. 124-125).

Marxism, therefore, judges, but is not judged. Its criteria are internal. Elsewhere, Fr. Bright makes light of philosophical incompatibilities in the most cavalier manner. 'Historical materialism', he informed readers of *The Tablet*, 'is merely a particular way of looking at things' (Letter, 13 September 1975). However, Fr. Bright is careful to explain that he does *not* believe that Christianity 'leads into Marxism' by a process of reasoning, or that Christianity entails Marxism. He rejects this procedure as contrary to Marx's doctrine that 'it is action that determines thought' (*What Kind of Revolution?* p. 124).

Yet the method that Fr. Bright is loath to use is widespread among Christians For Socialism. We have already seen that for Pietro Brugnoli, 'the logic of Christian faith' ought to lead one to embrace Marxism. One theorist has gone further still and defended the proposition that 'Marxism is not only not inconsistent with Christianity; Christianity is compatible only with Marxism' ('Can a Christian Be a Marxist?' Denys Turner, *New Blackfriars*, June 1975, pp. 244-253). Turner's case, which is argued with considerable charm, rests on the premise that 'capitalism' is such an unqualified evil that its rejection is the most urgent of all tasks. The premise is thus stated: 'The Church can never be a community under conditions of capitalism, because what the Church means by community it means by love, and what it means by love is Christ. And under capitalism community is not possible because love is not livable and thus Christ is not visible' (*ibid.*, p. 250). Turner has here adopted the characteristic Marxist doctrine that 'morality' is not possible under capitalism since you cannot draw straight lines in curved space. Morality begins only after the revolution. There can be no mistaking his meaning:

> The Christian must now be a Marxist because and only because there is no longer any issue in the world but one, the issue of being for or against the revolution of the capitalist world. For just so long as 'the world' is a specifically capitalist world, Marxism alone can define the *praxis* of the Christian. And this is because for just so long as the world is capitalist there is only one revolutionary *praxis*. That is not a doctrine of Christianity. It is just a fact which capitalism imposes (*ibid.*, p. 252).

Turner represents an extreme case, the culmination of a process which one can see developing in other Christian Marxists. First, narrow the focus so that one large black Manichaean evil fills the entire horizon. 'Capitalism' acts in this way in Turner's argument. It is never defined. None of the modifications that democratic countries have introduced to curb the harshness of capitalism are mentioned. The plain fact of continuing alienations in Communist countries remains unnoticed. It is as though we were dealing with the simplified figures of a medieval morality play, in which black-hearted capitalism struts the stage uttering cries of exploitation, while noble-hearted socialism is ready to confront him in the final eschatological scene. The way is then open to rejecting all those who do not agree with you as sunk in illusions. They are deluded, for example, in imagining that 'love is possible' in capitalist society. All the characteristics of ideological thinking are here conveniently gathered together.

There is as yet no satisfactory synthesis between Christianity and Marxism. One observer tartly observed that the Christian Marxists 'were wildly trying out combinations in the hope that they would hit upon the right one'. So far it has not been discovered, and the simple explanation may be that none is possible, that it is an attempt to square the circle. Of course words—'the wise man's counters and the money of fools'—can be stretched this way and that, and in every attempted synthesis there is a preliminary redefinition which stresses the revolutionary content of Christianity and the pacific and humanly fulfilling ideals of Marxism. Marxism gets the benefit of the doubt. It is seen in the lyrical terms of a British Communist, who wishes to remain anonymous:

> We envisage Communism as a classless society, where work becomes a pleasure, where the state (including the armed forces, police, etc.) can 'wither away', where war becomes a museum piece, where men and women reach full equality, where art (beauty) becomes a part of life, where the 'brotherhood of man' becomes a reality, where men and women can shed their alienation and become more 'truly human'. The watchword will be 'from each according to his ability, to each according to his need'.

There is nothing wrong with this vision, except that it nowhere exists. It verifies Herbert Spencer's definition of tragedy: 'A beautiful dream spoiled by ugly facts'. It could still be a pointer to the future, but it is not a description of the present.

In the present, one has to say that the 'mutual fruitfulness' said to exist between Christianity and Marxism has proved to be a one-way street. Christians embrace Marxism, and sometimes claim to revivify it with forgotten notions such as forgiveness and reconciliation, but so far Marxists have not welcomed their contribution. There is a path from Christianity to Marxism, but not from Marxism to Christianity. When Roger Garaudy announced his adherence to a form of Christian faith in 1975, he did not claim that his conversion was 'in the logic' of Marxism. On the contrary, he explained that he had come to believe in God, that for him this meant that 'man is more than man' and that faith can bring to socialism a transcendental and prophetic dimension without which it will remain deficient and underdeveloped (*Parole d'Homme*, Grasset, 1975). There is no record of any Marxist embracing Christianity as a result of a deeper study of Marxism; but many Christians have embraced Marxism, they claim, as a result of a deeper study of Christianity. The crucial, determining element in the supposed synthesis is therefore Marxism, and Christianity is subordinated to it.

Some Christian Marxists freely admit that they do not expect to make a contribution to Marxism. Their role is to prepare the Church to accept Marxism, or, in Hugo Assmann's words, 'to make a breach in the superstructure represented by traditional bourgeois values'. Assmann continues:

> In that sense, Christian revolutionary action has already been most effective: for the traditional concept of the ideal Christian as above all a man of 'peace' pacifically stationed within the existing order, quietly collaborating with the rules of the *status quo*, has virtually become a thing of the past (*Practical Theology of Liberation*, p. 139).

The editors of *Dialog* are equally frank. 'By deliberately remaining in the Church', they explain, 'and making use of its symbolic system and its institutional possibilities, a "chain reaction" will be set in motion which will transform both Church and society' (*Dialog*, 1974, 3, p. 197). This rather sibylline utterance, presented as a 'guideline for action', would seem to lend some justification to the right-wing fears of a Trojan Horse tactic, all the more when the *Dialog* editorial continues: 'The partial overlapping of the two realms will be deliberately taken as the basis for a paradigm realization of the unity of Christianity and socialism' (*ibid.*). In other words, Christians For Socialism cannot hope to persuade all Christians to become Marxists overnight, but they can point to the partial agreement between Christians and Marxists on *some* issues as an anticipation of eventual *full* agreement. Once Christians concede—as they must —that the world needs justice and fraternity, they are invited to embrace Marxism as the only embodiment of these aspirations.

When faced by Marxism in its multiple forms, Christians have a difficult task of *discernment*. 'The Church', says the pastoral constitution *Gaudium et Spes*, 'has always had the duty of scrutinizing the signs of the times and of interpreting them in the light of the Gospel' (4). Marxism is an ambiguous and ambivalent 'sign of the times': positively it expresses aspirations for a more just and equal society, but it is flawed by its incapacity to place checks on the abuse of power and its ideological totalitarianism. For this reason, the response of Christians should be neither unconditional acceptance nor unconditional rejection. I have been sufficiently critical of Marxism in this book to be able to say in conclusion that 'anti-communism' alone is a sterile and inadequate policy. Indeed it is not a policy at all so much as an alibi for the absence of a policy. Anti-communism can be a mirror image of that which it rejects, using the same authoritarian methods to root out all opposition and trampling on the deepest human aspirations. The role of the Church is not to propound a precise blueprint for the ordering of society. It is constantly to keep before mankind the criteria by which any system of ordering society must be judged. Where human rights are denied, where participation in government is non-existent, where the state behaves as though it originated values and determined morality, then the Church must declare its opposition clearly. It is the enemy of rationalizing ideologies, and it must combat them within itself as well. 'A world without God', said Gardavsky, 'would be clearer and easier to control' (*ibid.*,

p. 153). No doubt it would. But that is precisely why the sense of the living God as mankind's future and destiny can preserve us from all idolatry of the state and the Party, and at the same time open our eyes to the injustice and oppression which are no part of God's intention for mankind.

I used a quotation from Pierre Teilhard de Chardin at the end of Chapter 1. I conclude with another quotation from Teilhard which points towards the as yet unrealized vision of a synthesis between a transformed Marxism and a renewed Christianity:

> You speak of the attitude of Rome towards communism. I understand their approach very well as a defensive tactic. But I still regret that along with its excommunication Rome does not also publish a document . . . explaining that although the Church condemns communism in so far as it is materialist and atheist, in return she also understands and accepts communist aspirations to the extent that they indicate not merely a legitimate need for *well-being* but an irrepressible urge for *more-being*.

> Now this is precisely, in my view, the nub of the present difficulty. In Rome they see communism only as the product of social dissatisfaction, which they think can be brought to heel with a little more comfort and justice. Now in essence, if I am not mistaken, communism (a very bad term for what is really a neo-humanism) is the expectation of an ultra-humanity in all fields; it corresponds to a new faith and a new hope in man; and then, it could only be matched or surpassed by a Christianity in which faith in God has incorporated and sublimated the new human faith in the earthly future of humanity. . . .

> One can outline the situation in this way. One group (the traditionalist Christians) say 'Let us wait for Christ to return'. Another (the Marxists and their sympathisers) reply: 'Let us perfect humanity'. The third (the new Christians) think, 'In order that Christ might be able to return, let us

accomplish humanity on the earth'. But in Rome they don't yet see that 'faith in man' is a distinctly new element in the human soul; they don't feel it—they only see it as a fashion. That is the tragedy.

Meanwhile, those who feel deeply within themselves the conviction that ahead of us are not simply men, but rather a new man still to come, these, caught between a dead Stalinism and a Catholic authority which fails to understand them, form an evergrowing mass of 'displaced persons', 'wandering sheep', for whom Our Lord surely has great sympathy (Letter to Simone Beaulieu, 7 August 1949, published in *Bulletin d'Information et de Recherche*, 13 December 1967).

INDEX

Also published by Darton, Longman & Todd:

'*A Marxist Looks at Jesus* is both a scholarly and a strangely moving interpretation of the life and teachings of Jesus of Nazareth. It offers relevant and reverent insights into both the historical and contemporary significance of those teachings for Christians, Marxists, and a far wider world audience that shares in the heritage of the Judaic, Christian and Socialist traditions.'

Tony Benn

'. . . a dispassionate, highly intelligent, scholarly examination of Christianity in history. . . . it should be obligatory reading for any serious student of Christianity today.'

The Times

'This is the sort of book which raises one's eyes above the dogmas of philosophers or theologians, above the machinations of politicians or even statesmen, above the ululations of economists or ecologists or whoever and proudly proclaims: You are a man involved in a life bigger than you thought with a future which begins now and continues . . .

This is an exciting book.'

Books and Bookmen